Barbara was trying to juggle work, be an attentive parent, and take care of her husband's affairs—leaving her frazzled by the end of each day. It was all she could do to put dinner on the table each night. Diana began to throw daily tantrums while Joy withdrew.

Like many proceedings, the legal process went on for over one year. More than $7,500 of the small estate had been paid in legal expenses and two-thirds of the remaining amount—$45,000 in total—had been put into trust funds for the children. Alan's mother, who had never been fond of Barbara, attempted to gain the guardianship of those trust funds. She did not succeed, but the court assigned a court trustee—a complete stranger—to oversee the funds until the children reach age 21. This left Barbara just $22,500 to pay off funeral and other death-related debts and to help make up her monthly deficit.

Had Alan had a good estate plan, Barbara could have had access to the full $75,000 almost immediately after his death. While this would not have reduced the pain that Barbara and the two little girls felt, it would have greatly reduced the strain that they experienced. It would have made it possible to keep the children in their familiar home and provide Barbara a little time to recover and prepare for a better paying job.

TO PROPHESY IS EXTREMELY DIFFICULT—ESPECIALLY WITH RESPECT TO THE FUTURE.

—MARK TWAIN

No one likes to think about dying. Seventy percent of Americans die without a will or will replacement, according to **Consumer Reports.** Unquestionably, people just don't want to think about, talk about, or plan for death. Perhaps the greatest enemy of estate planning is procrastination! Many people do not fully grasp that they are not immortal and believe that they will have plenty of warning to do their estate planning. Subsequently, they lose many living benefits of estate and financial planning and leave their survivors with a mess.

Nine Excuses for Not Planning Your Estate

1. What is estate planning?
2. I don't see the need for an estate plan.
3. I don't plan on dying soon.
4. I don't want to pay for it.
5. I don't want to spend the time.
6. I don't want to deal with conflicting opinions.
7. I don't want to talk about money.
8. I don't want to ruin my children.
9. I don't trust my heirs.

The worries and costs of estate planning are minor compared to what our survivors go through when we die without a good estate plan.

Most people assume, wrongfully, that all of their personal and business assets, insurance and government benefits will automatically go to their heirs upon their death.

As statistics reveal, this type of story is not unique to Barbara and her children. Many people today ask whether they really need an estate plan. Do you need one? Ask yourself the following questions: If I were to fall ill or die, do I care about...

- Who will take care of my children or other dependents?
- Who makes decisions about my health and physical well-being?
- Who gets my property?
- Who gets my money?
- How much of my money goes to legal expenses and the government?
- How much strife and disagreement occurs between my heirs over my affairs?
- How much pain, anguish, difficulty and work my heirs have to go through to straighten out my affairs and manage my property?

If you answered yes to any one of the above questions, then you need an estate plan. Today, the means to create and leave behind a well-planned estate is available to almost everyone. Attorneys, accountants, and competent professionals can help you draw up the necessary documents, and there is a wealth of reading material in libraries, bookstores and on the internet to guide you through the process.

The point of estate planning is to pass along your assets—however great or small—to the persons or institutions you choose as directly, quickly, and with as little trouble and expense as possible. To do so, you must take certain steps or the law will dictate that your property be distributed in ways that may not be according to your wishes and will likely be at greater expense to your estate. With each year that passes, it becomes more critical to prepare or refine your estate plan. The most important thing is to get started—it is never too late and it is (almost) never too early! (See page 96.)

The most important thing to keep in mind is that preparing an estate plan is an act of love. It is also a means of ensuring that your estate enriches the lives of the people and institutions you care about.

Wills, Trusts & Estate Planning

Are you ready?

Two million people die each year in the United States. More than 70 percent of these people have not pre-planned for their funeral or put their affairs in order, let alone left a will or an estate plan in place. The following story is an example of the nightmare that can result.

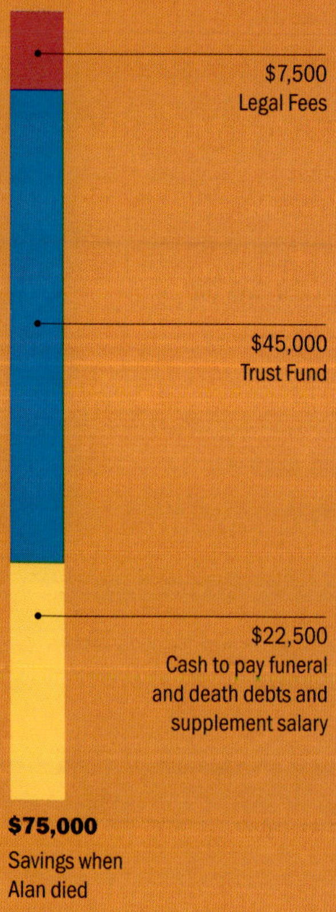

One cold snowy night, Alan, a 40 year-old father and store manager, was killed by a drunk driver while out Christmas shopping. He was survived by his 34 year old wife, Barbara and two beautiful daughters, Diana and Joy, ages 3 and 5.

The family had struggled a little over the years but were comfortable, living in a small town in Colorado. They had a modest savings of $75,000—money Alan had inherited from his grandmother—which they had been saving to buy a house. Alan, like the majority of the population, had not prepared an estate plan.

Alan's sudden death threw Barbara and the girls into a tailspin. Barbara had been a stay-at-home mother and had outdated work skills. Without Alan to provide for the family, she now had to find inexpensive childcare for the girls, and—while still deeply grieving her loss— find a job. She soon found work as an administrative assistant at a medical clinic earning $400 per week, less than half of what Alan had been earning. And since Alan's estate was held up in legal proceedings, Barbara could not access their savings. She had to leave the home they had rented for the last 5 years and move in with her sister, just to make ends meet. She and the two girls shared the guest bedroom.

An estate is your stuff. We all have an estate.

While for most people the word estate conjures up images of elegant mansions or massive accumulations of wealth, there is another kind of estate that we all have. Simply put, your estate is everything you own all or part of, less your debts. After you die, your estate becomes a legal entity, which is capable of owing or being owed money, and capable or incapable of meeting financial obligations.

Your estate is equal to your net worth—the value of your assets minus any debts. Assets in your estate can include any **real property,** bank accounts, investment accounts, stocks, bonds, mutual funds, insurance proceeds, retirement plans, and money owed to you, and **tangible personal property** such as jewelry, art, furniture, and cars. All liabilities are also taken into account, whether it is the mortgage on your house, your credit card balance, or the money you owe your uncle.

What exactly is an estate?

Real property is real estate—any land and the buildings on it.

Tangible personal property refers to your possessions, such as furniture, wedding rings, and even your pet dog.

What is estate planning?

A will is a document in which you leave instructions as to who will receive your assets after your death.

Beneficiaries are the people named to receive *bequests* in an estate plan. Beneficiaries may or may not be heirs, just as heirs may or may not be beneficiaries.

Bequests are the property left to beneficiaries in an estate plan.

Executors are named in a will to dispose of an estate.

Trusts are vehicles for holding assets for the benefit of one or more parties but which are managed by another (the trustee).

Trustees are named to manage a trust.

Administrator is title given to the person the court names to administer an estate in the absence of a will.

Heirs are the family members who would legally inherit your estate if you were to die without a will or other estate plan naming your *beneficiaries.*

Estate planning is the process of getting ready for the inevitable.

Estate planning is what you do to develop, protect, and plan your estate. Although most people think of estate planning as writing a **will,** it is usually much more. Good estate planning will reduce estate taxes and avoid delays. Estate planning is actually part of financial and life planning. These types of planning involve accumulating and preserving assets and income, preparing for the challenges you might face throughout your life and disposing of your estate after your death.

Estate planning starts with determining your financial objectives and includes a thorough inventory of your assets and liabilities. When planning your estate:

- Family objectives and circumstances must be considered and clearly discussed.
- Each asset, business agreement, property deed, insurance policy, or other property must be reviewed.
- Certain assets, such as closely held business interests or real property, may need to be formally appraised.
- Succession planning for your business (planning who will take over for you) and for the management of family assets will need to be reviewed and formalized. This should include an assessment of family relations, needs, and skills.
- Methods for long term preservation of your wealth, such as generational planning (skipping a generation and leaving your estate directly to grandchildren, thereby reducing your children's estates when they die) should be considered.
- Analysis of issues relative to you now while alive, such as future retirement and financial security issues, should be undertaken before any major decisions are implemented.
- A review of your current and future living expenses and cash flow sources should be included. A good estate plan will address concerns that are relevant now and will be in the future–such as medical and healthcare considerations.
- Income tax and estate tax planning should be incorporated throughout the plan.

Estate planning is the combination of financial and legal steps that provide peace of mind, not only to your **beneficiaries** later but to you (and your spouse) now. No two estate plans are or should ever be alike. There are no rights or wrongs when it comes to your feelings and the needs of your loved ones. While professionals can advise you of your options, only you can make the personal decisions necessary to truly customize your estate plan.

You can plan for who will administer your estate.

In a will, the person named to dispose of an estate according to your instructions, is called the **executor** or, in some states, a personal representative. If, instead of or in addition to a will, you have a **trust,** then the person named to manage the trust is called a **trustee.** If you have not left an estate plan, the person who is appointed by the court to perform the duties of managing your estate is called the **administrator** (or administratrix, if female), although some states also use the term personal representative in this case as well. Responsibilitites of the person (or persons) administering your estate include:

- Gathering assets
- Paying debts and expenses
- Filing the necessary income and estate tax returns and paying any taxes due
- Investing the estate assets prudently
- Distributing the assets as instructed in the will and/or trust, or, in the absence of any estate plan, in accordance with state intestacy laws.

Your **heirs** or beneficiaries may not have the qualities, skills and training which are desirable in an estate administrator. Possible other candidates include your attorney, accountant, a bank representative, or a trusted friend. Some jurisdictions (governed areas) impose additional requirements that the administrator must fulfill, such as living in the state, being a relative, or posting a surety bond (a type of insurance that would pay for any losses in the event of default or negligence).

Who will administer my estate?

Selecting an Executor

The person (or people) you choose to administer your estate plan should be trustworthy, sufficiently available, and capable of assuming responsibilities. You should always appoint a successor executor in the event your first choice is unavailable or dies before you. Usually close family members, especially if they are also a beneficiary, will serve as your executor without fees, but there may be some cases where paying fees has some tax advantages.

Administrators are appointed by the court to serve as an executor when someone dies without a will. Administrators are paid for their work by your estate. The fee is set by statute, and is commonly a percentage of the total estate.

You can appoint as many co-executors or co-trustees as you want. To avoid hurt feelings and conflict among children, parents sometimes appoint them all to administer the estate. However, this can be rather cumbersome.

A firm grasp of your current financial situation is the foundation for any sensible estate plan.

What can a good estate plan accomplish?

A good estate plan can...

Provide for the immediate family. Couples can provide, at minimum, enough money for the surviving spouse to continue living at the level to which they are accustomed. There are many stories of the family home or other valuable assets having to be sold to pay taxes, court fees, or living expenses after the death of a spouse. Individuals with dependent children can ensure that they keep a familiar roof over their children's heads, as well as provide for their education and upbringing.

Take some of the burden off the family. The more details you arrange ahead of time, the less your grieving relatives will have to deal with, in addition to losing you.

Provide for dependents. If you have family members whose lives might become more difficult without you, such as **minors,** disabled adult children, or elderly parents, you can ensure that their needs, both financial and physical, are addressed.

Get property to beneficiaries quickly. Your beneficiaries can receive their inheritance with fewer delays and less legal and governmental interference.

Plan for the possibility that you can't take care of yourself. What if you are **incapacitated?** A well-thought-out estate plan can help you prepare for the possibility that you will become unable to make medical, financial, or other personal decisions for yourself. You can pass on your wishes about health care and you can establish who will take care of your personal affairs, finances, or how your dependents, if you have any, will be cared for.

Allow you to choose the executors and trustees of your estate. Without an estate plan, the courts will decide who will oversee your estate. Your estate plan allows you to make the choice of someone you know and trust, who has all the qualifications and knowledge to successfully execute the disposition of your property. And you will have the opportunity to tell them personally what your intentions are, leaving less to guesswork.

Minors are individuals who are below the age when full legal and civil rights can be legally exercised. They are said to be below the age of majority—usually 18 or 21, depending on the state.

Incapacity is the lack of ability, power, or fitness to carry out your own wishes. You are 4 to 7 times more likely to become incapacitated than to die in any one year.

Permit you to support a favorite cause. Your plan gives you the freedom to support religious, educational, and other charitable causes, either during your lifetime or upon your death, which can, in turn, possibly save you money in taxes also.

Minimize expenses. A thoughtfully prepared estate plan can arrange the distribution of your assets such that legal costs remain low. Depending on the size of your estate, this can mean thousands of dollars more for your beneficiaries.

Reduce estate taxes. A good estate plan can ensure that the maximum allowed by law goes to your beneficiaries and the minimum amount of tax to the government. Larger estates can save hundreds of thousands of dollars.

Ensure that a business continues smoothly. All too often, a business owner dies and his family or his business partners are unable to continue or are forced to dismantle the company to pay debts and estate taxes or legal fees. You can provide for an orderly **succession** and continuation of your business through estate planning, whether a family member wishes to continue it or not.

Provide funeral and burial plans. Making these arrangements in advance can free loved ones from burdensome tasks immediately after your death, and can almost always save signifi cant amounts of money.

Provide for specific use and distribution of your estate. Only with an estate plan are you able to exercise real control over who benefits from your estate, how much they benefit, and when they can receive the benefits (only some estate plan tools offer this flexibility). Similarly, only with an estate plan can you specify who will *not* benefit from your estate.

Avoid family squabbles. Having no plan or a poor plan may lead to disagreement, bitterness, and lawsuits. Even if you can't or don't want to decide who gets what, you can create a neutral binding method for determining distribution of your property after your death.

An estate plan can include giving tax deductible gifts before your death, which can reduce both your income taxes while alive and estate taxes after death.

Succession planning can legally establish who steps into your shoes in running your business and even, to some degree, what actions they may or may not take.

If you have made funeral and other arrangements, be sure to tell someone you trust about them and leave the necessary information in an easy- to-find spot.

Family disputes are not always over valuable property. If different family members have deep emotional attachments to family heirlooms, no matter what their monetary value, fighting can become fierce.

Can I do without an estate plan?

Maybe. But probably not.

You can do without an estate plan if you have no assets, no liabilities, no responsibilities, no concern for how you or your estate are disposed of, and no concern for what your survivors must deal with after your death. Otherwise, you should have an estate plan.

What if I only have a small estate? If you have a small estate, perhaps your estate plan can be less elaborate, but it will still minimize the chaos and trouble your survivors must go through and maximize the amount of the estate they receive. Smaller estates can very easily be entirely eaten up with legal costs and other related expenses, making creative estate planning even more important.

Doesn't having beneficiaries designated for all of my accounts do the same thing as an estate plan? Most of us feel quite satisfied when we have established retirement accounts, pensions, investments, or insurance policies with **designated beneficiaries.** But this kind of "planning" can result in dramatic estate tax liability and could seriously affect your intentions for the distribution of your property. Why? Because no matter who you might designate as your beneficiaries, the pension and insurance proceeds (often in the high thousands of dollars), will be included in the total value of your estate for the purposes of calculating any estate taxes due. But the person(s) who receive those proceeds may not be required to contribute to the taxes to be paid. Instead, the person(s) receiving the remainder of the estate will be forced to pay all the taxes out of their portion if those who received the pension and insurance proceeds do not volunteer to contribute to the taxes.

Designated beneficiaries are the people you name as your beneficiaries on your insurance policy or retirement accounts.

For example, imagine that your uncle died and left his home to you, valued at $500,000. Your uncle also left a life insurance policy designating your aunt as a beneficiary. After allowances, his taxable estate totaled $350,000. Unless the estate plan provided that the estate taxes be apportioned or divided against all assets, you would be responsible for the taxes on the $350,000 (which could total $100,000).

Just designating beneficiaries on all your accounts can result in estate liabilities that undermine your intentions.

Your aunt would not be required to pay any of it. In a case such as this, an estate plan can provide some continuity that deals with the overall estate, addressing all pieces of the entire puzzle.

What if I have no heirs? If you have no legal heirs, you want your entire estate to go to the state, and you do not care who is in charge or how your personal property is dealt with, then you do not need an estate plan. When you die without an estate plan, the courts take over; in the event that there are no legal heirs, they cannot and do not leave any part of your estate to your favorite charity or cause or to any friends you leave behind. It all goes to the state to dispose of as they see fit.

What if I do not want to leave anything to my heirs? If you do not want to leave anything to your legal heirs, you definitely need an estate plan, for if you die without one, your estate will automatically go to your legal heirs, according to a standard state-created formula. Only a well-worded estate plan can prevent one or more of your legal heirs from receiving a portion of your estate.

FAILING TO PLAN IS PLANNING TO FAIL.

—ANONYMOUS

The person who doesn't make an estate plan is in illustrious company. Famous people who died without one include Abraham Lincoln, Andrew Johnson, and U.S. Grant, as well as Howard Hughes and Pablo Picasso.

What happens if I have no estate plan?

You create a mess when you die with a missing, outdated, or defective estate plan.

When you die without leaving a will or some other type of written estate plan, you die **intestate.** When you die intestate, the law takes over and directs who will take charge of your estate and how your property will be distributed—in effect, writing the will you failed to make. While laws are written to be as fair and equitable as possible, they are the same for everybody and rarely match what you would have chosen to do yourself. The law is based on general principles for the guardianship of children, the rights of relatives, and the management of the estate.

Your home or business may be sold or even bankrupted to meet debts and expenses. Your family may end up needing emergency assistance just to survive, while the court makes decisions about your estate.

The courts will decide who will take charge of your dependents and their finances, if you are single or divorced and have dependents. And those who do take charge will be doing so without the benefit of your instructions or knowing your wishes in regard to the care of your dependents.

The court will pick the administrator of your estate. Generally speaking, the surviving spouse has the first right to be appointed. In some cases, where two-thirds of an individual's estate has gone to children from a previous marriage, for example, this might not be desirable. If your spouse has pre-deceased you, then the general rule is that adult children have equal right to be appointed—and sometimes they are all jointly appointed. If they all do not agree on matters, every step they need to take could result in costly and inefficient administration of the estate.

The administrator's actions are limited by the laws of the county or state in which he or she is appointed. To sell property, satisfy claims or to distribute the estate, he or she must first seek the court's authorization and

Intestate comes from Latin. In means not. Testate comes from the latin word testatus, past participle of testari, which means to make a will.

Dying Intestate

Each of the 50 states has laws that prescribe, in great detail, what happens to a citizen's property if there is no estate plan. These laws are generally referred to as **statutes of descent and distribution** or as **statutes of intestate succession.**

If you die intestate, your estate will be distributed according to state law. No matter what, each of your children will share the estate equally. No special arrangements can be made for a child with special needs, or for the one adult child who stood by all her life caring for you, while another one might have been raised by a previous spouse and you had not seen her in 12 years.

the cost of each proceeding must be paid for out of the estate. While the limitations on the administrator are to protect the estate, they can also cost the estate money and the beneficiaries grief. For instance, administrators may be restricted to specific types of investments. So, if the estate consisted only of high-grade common stock, for example, but the law does not permit full investment in common stock, the administrator would have to sell some of the stock or risk personal liability. And if the asset that must be disposed of is the family business, the business and surviving family may suffer as a result.

Expenses will be greater. When there is no estate plan, the cost of administering an estate is usually greater. For instance, the cost of hiring legal professionals to take the estate through the court system, which is required for all estates without a plan, is taken out of the estate. Also, in most states, the administrator appointed by the court must purchase a bond. This bond is to protect beneficiaries and creditors should the administrator mishandle the estate. The premiums must, however, be paid out of the estate.

There may be unnecessary taxes. Dying without an estate plan means leaving things to chance. Even with larger estates, an estate plan allows you to leave your spouse your entire estate without triggering estate taxes. This is not true, however, for other heirs. When children exist and you die intestate, your spouse may receive no more than one-half or one-third of your estate. Or, if you die intestate and your spouse receives more than you would have left him or her in an estate plan designed to minimize overall taxes on both your estates, he or she may end up with too much in his or her own estate, making it unnecessarily subject to taxes when he or she dies. If, in the absence of a spouse or children, your parents become your heirs, they too might have preferred the funds go to another family member whose own estate was smaller and not taxable. There is waste instead of savings. It is easy to see how tax savings are one of the primary reasons for estate planning.

Both Spouses Should Have an Estate Plan

It is not enough for just one spouse to have an estate plan. To do it properly, both spouses should plan together, so that no matter who dies first, the property is passed on as smoothly as possible and with the least amount of taxes. Even if both spouses died together, if the one who had the estate plan died just minutes before the other, the estate would legally pass to the one who died last—who would in turn, die intestate and subject to intestacy laws.

One man, believing his wife would outlive him, put everything in her name. In fact, she died first without an estate plan, and he had to share his own property with a distant niece of hers whom they had not seen in 20 years.

To neglect, at any time, preparation for death, is to sleep on your post at a siege.

—Samuel Johnson

Your estate may go to unintended beneficiaries. The intestacy laws establish a pecking order for your heirs. While the laws vary from state to state, usually your spouse and children will receive property first. Your grandchildren are generally next in line followed by your parents, siblings, nieces and nephews, and cousins.

If you are single, your estate would probably go to your parents, your siblings and then nieces and nephews and then cousins, depending on who was still alive.

If you are married and have children, your spouse's share of your estate may be smaller than you would have intended. Depending on the state, your spouse will not receive the entire estate, as you would expect, but only one-third to one-half of your half of your joint estate. In some states, your estate will be shared equally between your grieving spouse and your children. If you have 4 children, that will mean your spouse will only receive one-fifth of the estate! The children's money will be put into trusts which the children will not have full access to until they reach the age of majority—18 to 21 years of age, depending on the state—at which point they will have complete control over the funds. In the meantime, if your spouse needs to access that money to care for the children, he or she would have to get the court's permission to use it and might be restricted from using it to provide for the children as he or she thinks best. Even if your spouse is appointed guardian, he or she will have to account to the court for every dollar spent—and will be subject to judicial supervision until all the children are grown. This can create a great hardship for both your spouse and children. The smaller the estate, the greater the hardship.

If you are married and have no children, you may assume that upon your death your half of the marital property would automatically go to your spouse. But this will not be the case. Often the surviving spouse must share the estate with the deceased spouse's parents,

I AM READY TO MEET MY MAKER, BUT WHETHER MY MAKER IS PREPARED FOR THE GREAT ORDEAL OF MEETING ME IS ANOTHER MATTER.

—WINSTON CHURCHILL

Stuck In Trusts?

Without a plan, most states will divide your estate with a portion to your spouse and the rest to your kids. The children's money will be put into a trust where your spouse cannot access it.

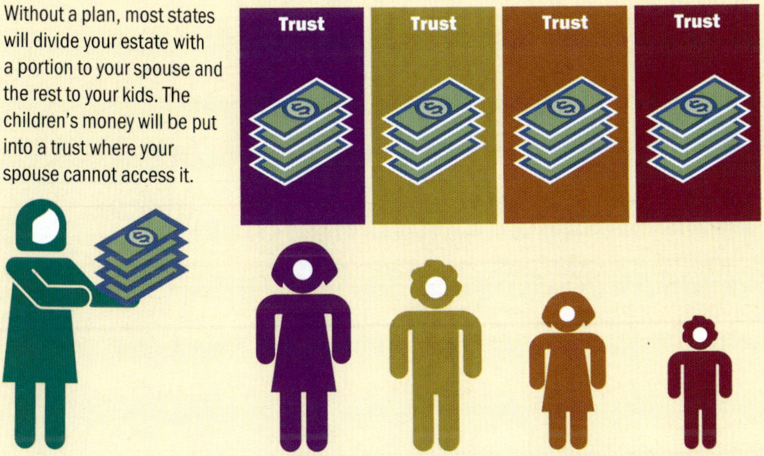

brothers and sisters and even nieces and nephews, whom they may not even know.

If you have no living blood relatives, your property will pass to the state. It is too bad if you have a favorite charity, a dear friend, or longtime companion you wanted to provide for—the state will get your entire estate.

If you have not already created an estate plan, it is advisable to decide to do so now—as if death were imminent—to cover both present needs and the needs of the foreseeable future. It can always be changed if you change your mind about something later (unless you create an irrevocable trust—see page 60). But if it is not made now, it may never be—and your property will be partially or wholly eaten up by unnecessary expenses, and distributed, perhaps, to unintended beneficiaries. And your loved ones, your survivors, will be facing the trials and tribulations of managing your estate.

It's not that I'm afraid to die, I just don't want to be there when it happens.

—Woody Allen

What is probate?

Probate is the process of legally passing ownership of property from a deceased person to his or her heirs or beneficiaries.

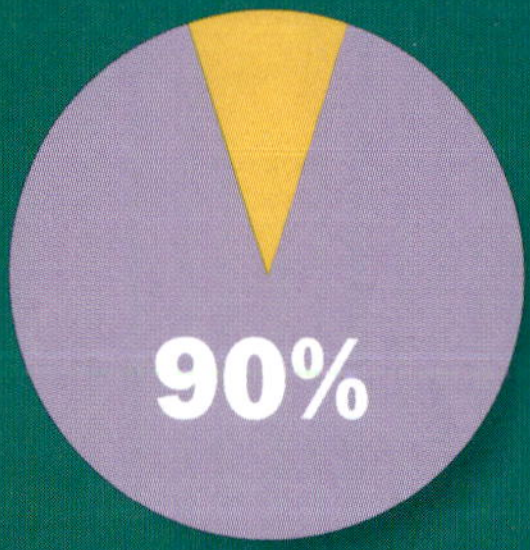

The estates of more than 90% of Americans with wills end up in probate court.

Probate courts administer the process. Keeping the property in your estate out of probate court should be one of your estate planning goals. Probate courts have been a part of our legal heritage for centuries. Every county in every state in the United States has its own probate system. In some places, it is called surrogate or common court.

Probate must be used to oversee the distribution of property according to the terms of a will, or the contents of an estate that has no will or will substitute. Although both wills and estates with no plans are handled through probate, estates without a plan demand extra handling, since there is no guidance from the decedent. There is nothing you can do with your will to allow it to bypass probate, although there are ways to keep property from passing through probate (see page 21).

Probate is time-consuming and can be costly. According to recent surveys, probate can take anywhere from six months to many years, the average time span being 15 months. Another study revealed that 22% of cases in probate were still open after three years. Only 20% were closed within 6 months. The cost of probate ranged from 4% to 54% of the gross estate.

Chapter 2

What happens in probate court?

Probate court appraises, assigns, files, and distributes your estate.

Delivering the deceased person's property into the hands of his or her heirs or beneficiaries is actually only one of the many tasks assigned to probate and, in fact, really doesn't occur until the end of the court proceeding.

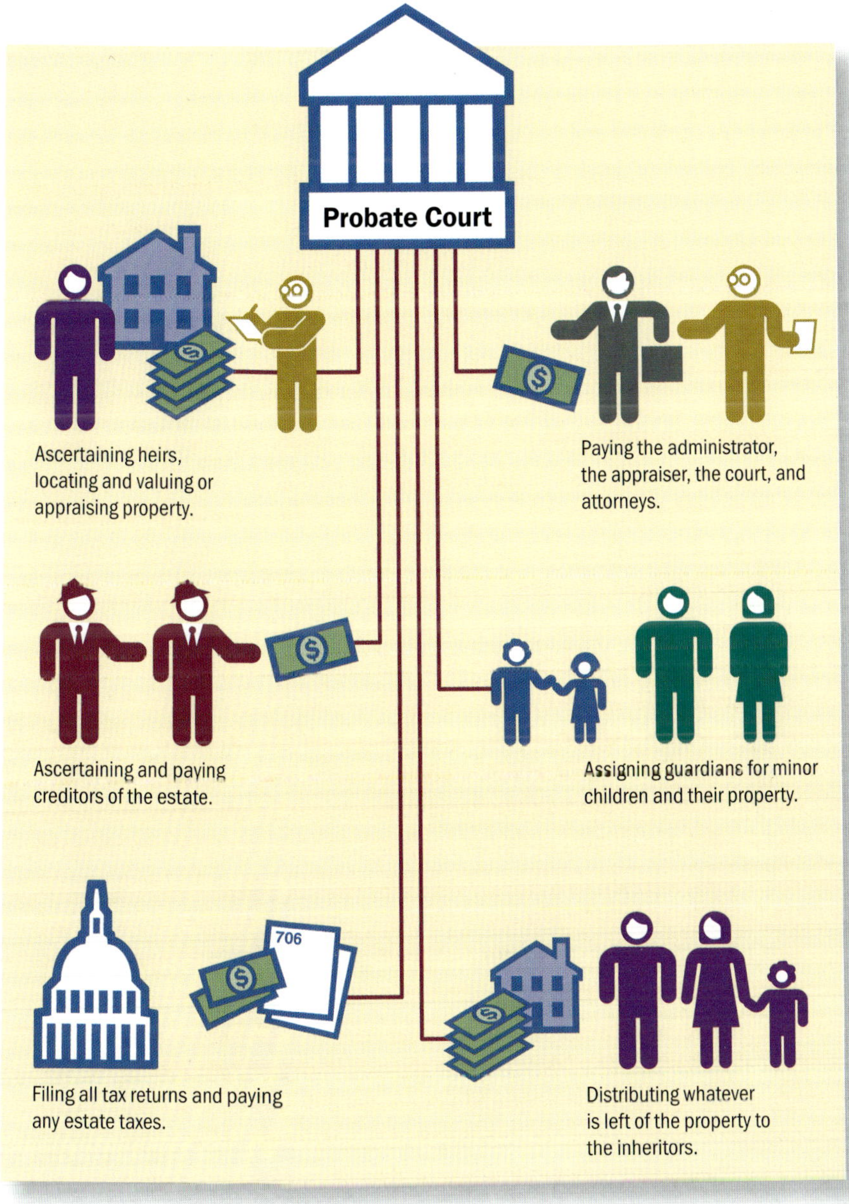

Probate comes from the Latin words probatum and probare, which means to examine, demonstrate as good, or prove.

Who is responsible for undertaking probate activities? The **probate** agent—the administrator/administratrix (in the case of no estate plan), the executor/executrix (in the case of a will), or the personal representative, as they are called in some states—is largely responsible for accomplishing these tasks. Sometimes when there is a will, and more often when there is not, the property has not been prepared for passing on to heirs. The administrator must play detective, finding and valuing the deceased's property and preparing all of the related paperwork. It took the deceased a lifetime to accumulate wealth, and more often than not, the books were kept upstairs—in their memories.

How are creditors found and paid? Before beneficiaries or heirs can receive anything, creditors must be found and paid. Finding, sorting out, and paying creditors of an estate can be frustrating and difficult if the deceased did not keep the financial records in an orderly fashion. Any problems involving creditors can hold up the distribution of the estate to inheritors. Administrators collect papers and mail to determine the debts of the deceased. They will also advertise, making a public announcement that creditors should come forward now.

Weaknesses in the Probate System

In general, the probate process is considered excessively bureaucratic. Its weaknesses can be summarized as follows:

1. Probate is complex and full of red tape
2. Probate is expensive
3. All of your affairs handled in probate are open to public scrutiny
4. Probate is time-consuming
5. Real control over your estate is held by the judge

Probate agents and probate lawyers are generally considered, according to the laws of most states, first-class creditors. They get paid first—before other creditors and even before the state or Federal government gets paid any taxes due.

Where does the money come from to pay creditors and taxes? If there is not enough cash available, assets might have to be sold to pay the creditors or taxes. What should and should not be liquidated can become a real source of disagreement. (See pages 32–33 for more specifics in this area.)

What about my dependents? If minors are involved, guardians are assigned. In most states, assets from the remaining estate are managed by state custodians. The courts will continue to stay involved until the dependents reach adulthood; in the case of adult beneficiaries who are mentally incompetent, the court might stay involved for their entire lifetime. In the event that a will already established trusts and trustees, the court gives them the stamp of approval and the necessary property and paperwork to carry out their duties.

The surviving spouse and children often find that they must petition the probate court to obtain access to funds that they need for ordinary living expenses. Every such petition must contain details and justification for the distribution, and every such petition is part of the public record. Aside from exposing the details of an estate to public scrutiny and review, the heirs must also reveal details of their own affairs in their petitions for release of the decedents' assets.

Changes in the Probate System

Some years ago, the American Bar Association recommended that every state revise its probate code because probate court had become bureaucratic and unwieldy. Not many states really made any changes based on the recommendation, and in the United States today, probate is considered by many to be one of the most agonizing and expensive experiences in which an individual can participate.

A MAN WHO DOES NOT PLAN LONG AHEAD WILL FIND TROUBLE RIGHT AT HIS DOOR.

—Confucius

How much will my estate have to pay for probate?

5 to 10 percent of your estate will go to pay for probate.

Because probate is not a simple legal process, survivors usually must rely on an attorney, as well as the administrator/executor to guide them through the legal maze. Subsequently, the estate must not only pay for the services of the administrator or executor, but they usually must also pay an attorney. The fees allowed for administrators or executors are usually established by state law, although they may be reviewed and awarded by the probate judge.

Probate costs generally run from 5% to 10% of the **gross estate,** depending on the size of the estate. The larger the estate, the lower the percentage. The greatest percentage of probate cost burden is borne by smaller estates. One study revealed that the greatest impact of probate costs was on estates of $100,000 or less. Many small estates have been almost entirely consumed by legal fees.

Gross estate is the fair market value of the estate, with no deductions or allowances for debts or liabilities such as mortgages.

Additional costs or losses may be incurred while an estate awaits completion of the probate process. Stock values have been known to deteriorate, and valuable businesses, built through years of hard work, could falter and die.

Probate Lawyers Fees

Probate attorneys receive annually, in total, fees of 1.6 billion dollars, according to an AARP estimate. This does not include court costs, appraiser's fees, and other types of costs.

Can my estate avoid probate?

Probate can be avoided through proper estate planning techniques.

While a will does not avoid probate, it usually makes the probate process easier than if there is no estate plan at all. There are, however, other estate planning techniques that can avoid probate altogether. The most popular general planning tool is the **inter vivos** or living trust (see page 70), while more specific tools include life insurance (see page 101) and retirement plans, joint tenancies (see page 37), designated beneficiaries, and pay-on-death (POD) or transfer-on-death accounts (see page 52), all of which will be addressed in more detail later in this book.

Everyone should be warned that the process of settling an estate when there has been inadequate or no planning can be extremely costly, time-consuming, and heartbreaking. Grown men and women have been known to cry over the frustration of probate. Relationships can be harmed or destroyed. Survivors devote valuable time to settling the probate estate, sometimes to the detriment of their own business affairs or families. It is only after the months or years of the probate process is complete that survivors can really begin to make a fresh start. The good news is that none of this frustrating process is necessary—with proper estate planning.

Although Marilyn Monroe died in debt, her estate earned over $1.6 million dollars in movie royalties over the 18 years after her death. At the end of that period, probate costs had eaten up over $1,000,000 of it.

THE COST OF PROBATE EXPANDS TO CONSUME THE MONEY AVAILABLE.

—Legal Scholar

What are estate taxes?

Estate taxes are amounts your estate pays to Federal and state governments on your estate, before anything remaining in the estate is transferred to your heirs or beneficiaries. The following story demonstrates how the burden of estate taxes can be very costly.

Judy's Dad Dies

One attorney's client, Judy, came to him hoping to avoid the mistakes her parents had made. Her father had died, leaving a will. He gave $100,000 outright to her, in cash, and left the balance of the estate, valued at about $1,400,000, to his wife (tax free because of the unlimited marital deduction). There was also no estate tax on Judy's $100,000, due to the $600,000 estate tax exemption which was in place at the time. Judy's mother's portion consisted of a nice home and some commercial real estate that her father purchased long ago at very modest prices. Since Judy had all the cash and her mother had little source of income, Judy felt obliged to pay the probate fees of $46,300, leaving her with just over half of what her father had intended for her.

Unfortunately, Judy's mother did not seek help with her estate plan and died eleven years later. In her will, she left several personal items valued at $125,000 to a new husband and all of her real estate to Judy, which now, due to changes in the economy and a series of poor financial decisions, had a fair market value of $1,050,000 and mortgages of $250,000. The properties had marginal cash flow and Judy had no ability to pay the probate fees of $50,350. Furthermore, she now had tax to pay, since the amount she inherited was above the estate tax credit. Judy could not pay the tax, so the court held an auction of several of the real estate parcels, which had been in her family for many years. Judy didn't need her new attorney to confirm what she already knew. There was no reason why her inheritance should have cost her personal, out-of-pocket expenses of $96,650 in probate fees, plus leaving her with no resources to pay the estate tax of $120,250. Careful planning by her parents would have avoided probate expenses entirely and would have left Judy with almost enough cash to pay the estate tax.

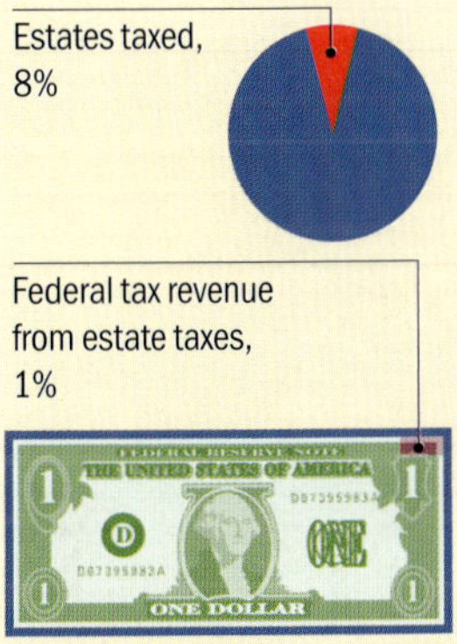

Uncle Sam receives his portion of an estate before the beneficiaries do. Only about 8% of estates owe any taxes, yet estate taxes generate about 1% of Federal tax revenue. The bulk of estate taxes are collected on the largest 1% of estates, but many more estates are still required to file federal estate tax returns.

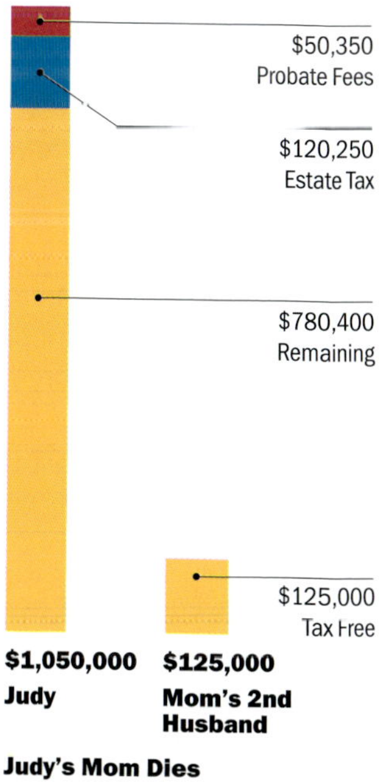

What makes up my taxable estate?

Federal Estate Tax Laws are written in the Internal Revenue Code (IRC) which can be found in Volume 26 of the United States Code which is the official collection of all federal statutes. More information about federal estate and gift taxes can be found in IRS publication no. 448 Federal and Estate Gift Taxes, which is available for free at many IRS offices.

Fair market value is the amount property would sell for, should it be sold.

If you are married, how you own property and the laws of your state can affect what part of your joint property is part of your individual estate.

Property and assets, less debts and standard deductions, make up your taxable estate.

- If you are a U.S. citizen or resident, then all assets located in the United States and some assets located outside of the United States, if they produce income for you, are considered part of your estate.
- If you own property outside of the U.S., it may be subject to estate taxes in that country.
- If you live in one of the few states that impose death taxes in addition to federal estate taxes, property located in those states may be subject to a state tax.
- If you are not a citizen or resident of the U.S. but have property in the U.S., that property could also subject to estate taxes.
- If you have any debts, they can then be deducted from the total sum of your assets, along with any death-related costs your estate incurs after your death.
- Standard deductions may be available to reduce your taxable estate, including the Unified Credit, the Unlimited Marital Deduction, and charitable deductions. (See page 75-79 for details.)

How will my estate be appraised after my death for taxation purposes? When assets transfer at death, they are valued at **fair market value.** Debts and liabilities are based on actual amounts you owe. If you owe any property other than cash, then it too would be valued at fair market value.

Finding the fair market value of property such as stocks, bonds, bank accounts, treasury bills, etc. can be relatively easy. However, evaluating property such as real estate, privately owned businesses, equipment, machinery and personal effects can be a very difficult task. You will save time and money for your estate if you keep well-marked receipts, bookkeeping records, and other documents showing the actual cost of items.

Who will appraise my estate? Assuming your estate is not large enough to warrant hiring a tax accountant, various parties will be involved in calculating the value of your estate, depending on your estate planning:

- If you die without an estate plan, then a court-appointed appraiser will charge your estate a fee based on a percentage of the property appraised.
- If you leave a will, your named executor will select the appraiser.
- If you leave a trust, the successor trustee (the trustee appointed in the trust to take over after your death) will select the appraiser, but the court will not have to approve this choice.
- If you leave all of your property by joint tenancy (see page 37), then the surviving joint tenant(s) will appraise the amount and file tax returns or pay taxes if they are due.

The Federal government does not get involved in property appraisal although it can challenge and audit estates just as in the case of income tax returns. The courts will decide the value of property if there is disagreement between your administrator and the IRS. In some states that impose estate taxes, the states do official appraisals as part of the system.

If you have a large estate which includes many assets, such as real estate, art and small businesses, for instance, appraising the value of your estate can be tricky. An experienced certified public accountant (CPA) with estate tax experience, or an estate planning attorney specialist, or both would be of invaluable help in navigating this path.

If beneficiaries intend to sell any property shortly after receiving it from your estate and the amount they sell it for is considerably more than the amount it is valued at for estate tax purposes, they may find themselves paying capital gains taxes on the profit they earn.

Valuation Dates

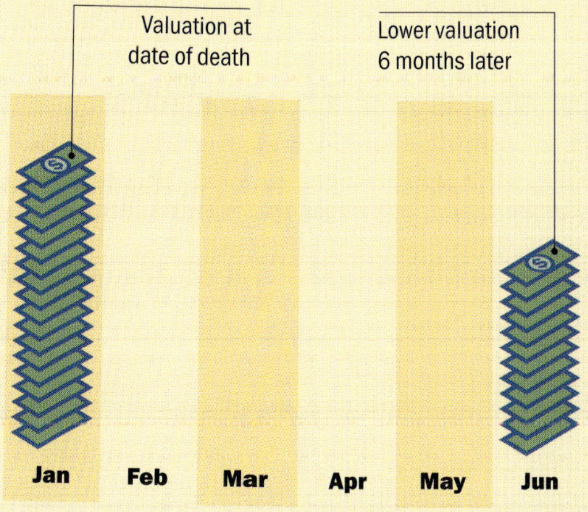

The law permits the value of your estate to be calculated at one of two dates: the date of your death or six months later—this is called the alternate valuation date. One date might be more desirable than another if the value of assets have substantially changed over the 6 month period. The date selected applies to all assets. You cannot choose one date for some assets and not others. If, during the six month period, any assets are sold, they must be valued at the actual amount they sold for.

What's the difference between inheritance taxes and estate taxes?

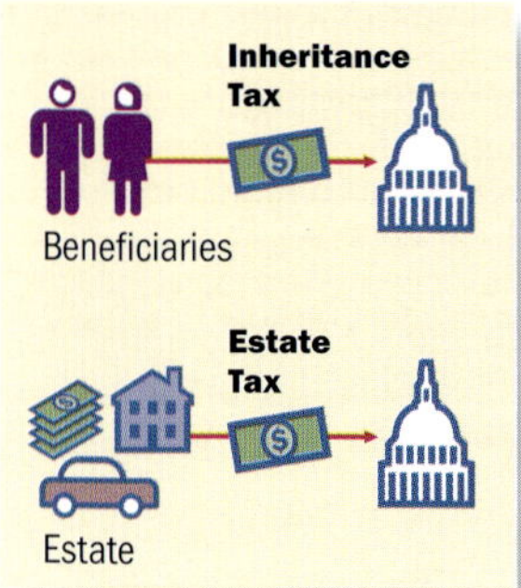

Estate taxes are paid by the estate; inheritance taxes must be paid by beneficiaries.

While heirs do not have to pay income taxes on the amounts they inherit (although they must pay income taxes on any income the inheritance produces) in some states, inheritance taxes are charged.

Inheritance taxes are not paid by your estate but by the people who inherit the estate. The inheritance tax rates vary from state to state, and get higher as the inheritance gets larger. The tax rates also vary depending on the relationship of the beneficiary to the deceased. The closest relation—a spouse, for instance—is taxed the least, while non-relatives are taxed at the highest rates. The rates range from 1% to 32%. There are some exemptions, which also vary depending on the relationship of the beneficiary to the deceased.

States With Inheritance Taxes

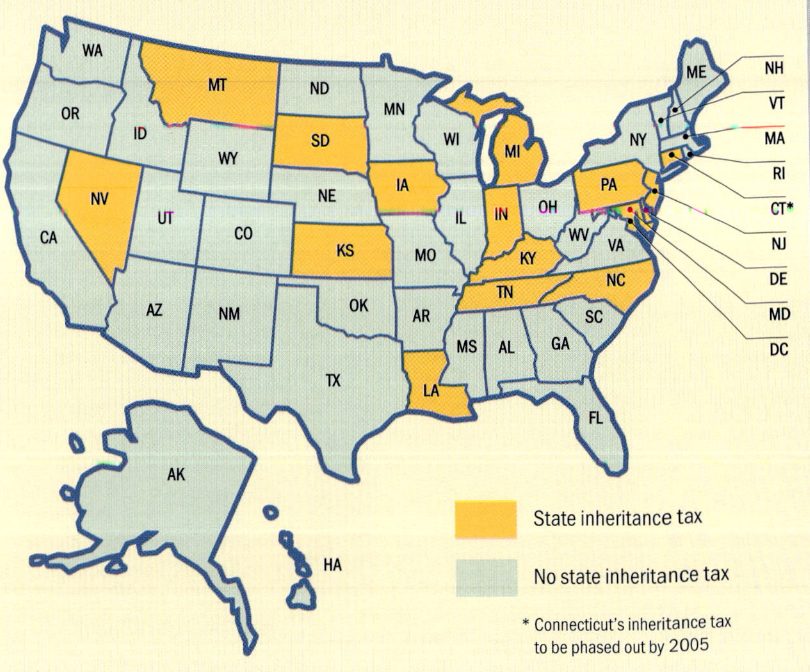

Are there any standard deductions to reduce estate taxes?

Standard deductions your estate may qualify for...

- **The unified credit.** You are permitted to leave up to the **exemption equivalent** of property to anybody you wish–estate tax free. In the year 2000, the exemption equivalent is $675,000 and this creates a tax savings or unified credit of $258,500. However, once an estate goes over $10,000,000, the unified credit is gradually phased out, and is entirely eliminated for estates over $21,040,000. (See tax table on page 29.)
- **The unlimited marital deduction.** Your spouse can receive an unlimited amount of your estate, completely free of estate tax. Please note that if the surviving spouse is not a U.S. citizen, he or she is not allowed the unlimited marital deduction, unless he or she becomes a naturalized citizen within 9 months of your death. (However, there are trusts that do allow, in these instances, for unlimited marital deductions. See page 75.) Unmarried couples cannot take advantage of this deduction.
- **The charitable deduction.** All property donated to a tax-exempt charity can be deducted from your taxable estate. The charity to which you intend to make a gift must have tax-exempt status. Most tax-exempt charities are 501(c)3 corporations.

How do I know if my estate will have to file an estate tax return? While it is more difficult to really calculate potential estate taxes due, it is a little easier to determine if a return must be filed. Form 706 must be filed if your gross estate (your assets before any expenses or liabilities are subtracted) exceed the exemption equivalent amount applicable in the year of your death. For this reason there are many times when a return must be filed even if taxes are not ultimately payable, due to deductions and exemptions. Form 706 should be prepared by a tax expert. It is not an easy form to complete. This federal estate tax return is due within 9 months of your death.

Exemption equivalent is an amount equal to the credit your estate can take according to the Internal Revenue Code Section 2010. This exemption is $675,000 in 2000 and will increase by various increments each year until it reaches the amount of $1,000,000 in the year 2006.

If your estate plan was created before 1981, it should be changed as soon as possible, to take advantage of the unlimited marital deduction. Estate plans created before September 1981 cannot take advantage of it.

The unlimited marital deduction can be a tax trap. Although no estate taxes are due when your estate passes to your spouse, your estate will increase the size of the estate of your surviving spouse, and if it goes over his or her $675,000 estate tax exemption, taxes will be due when he or she dies. For this reason, finding ways to also utilize your own unified credit is advisable.(See Living Trusts on page 61.)

How do I estimate what my estate's tax liability will be?

Federal Estate Tax Rates

Federal estate taxes were first seriously imposed in 1916 and had a maximum rate of 10%, as compared to today's maximum rate of 60%. Historically, tax rates have risen to as much as 70%, determined by congressional action.

Estimating your estate's tax liability.

Given that assets change in value over time, it is impossible to truly predict what your estate will be worth, and therefore what estate taxes might be payable when you die, but you can get an idea whether your estate will be subject to taxes or not.

How to estimate your Federal estate tax liability:

1. Estimate the value of what you own. . . . . $

   Don't forget to include the proceeds of your life insurance (unless you have a life insurance trust, see page 83), any annuities or retirement plans. (See page 34 on what makes up your estate.)

2. Enter the amount you owe . . . . $

3. Subtract line 2 from line one. **This is your net estate** . . . . $

4. Enter the amount you intend to give to your spouse. . . . . $
   *If your spouse is not a U.S. citizen, do not enter **0**.*

5. Enter the amount you intend to leave to tax-exempt charities . . . . $

6. Enter the estate tax equivalent exemption—the unified credit . . . . $
   Enter $675,000 for the year 2000 (see page 71 for exemption applicable in future years).

7. Add lines 4, 5, and 6. **This is your total deduction** . . . . $

8. Subtract line 7 from line 3. **This is your taxable estate**. . . . . $
   If your deductions do not reduce your estate to zero, estate taxes will be due. Check the estate tax table at right to determine what federal estate tax rate would be applicable. Use the middle columns, as the unified credit has been applied within this formula.

Federal Estate Tax Table

How to Use the Tax Table.

Taxes are calculated on assets within each range and then added up. For example, if all deductions and exemptions have been taken into consideration and there is $175,000 left to be taxed, the first $75,000 will be taxed at 37% and the remaining $100,000 will be taxed at 39%. So estate taxes on a $175,000 taxable estate would be $27,750 (37% of $75,000) plus $39,000 (39% of $100,000) for a total of $66,750.

Estate Value before Unified Credit	Taxable Estate Value (Estate Value less Unified Credit)	Tax Percentage applied to Taxable Estate Value
$ 0– $ 675,000	$ 0	0%
$ 675,001– $ 750,000	$ 1– $ 75,000	37%
$ 750,001– $ 1,000,000	$ 75,001– $ 325,000	39%
$ 1,000,001– $ 1,250,000	$ 325,001– $ 575,000	41%
$ 1,250,001– $ 1,500,000	$ 575,001– $ 825,000	43%
$ 1,500,001– $ 2,000,000	$ 825,001– $1,325,000	45%
$ 2,000,001– $ 2,500,000	$ 1,325,001– $1,825,000	49%
$ 2,500,001– $ 3,000,000	$ 1,825,001– $2,325,000	53%
$ 3,000,001– $10,000,000	$ 2,325,001– $9,325,000	55%
$10,000,001–$21,595,000	*	60%
$21,595,000 and up	$21,595,000 and up	55%

Examples

An estate valued at $500,000 pays $0 tax.

An estate valued at $1,000,000 pays $125,250 tax.

An estate valued at $5,000,000 pays $2,170,250 tax.

Tax rates vary with the size of the estate. The rate increases as the value of the estate goes up. See the table above for specific numbers.

* The unified credit is gradually phased out for estates over $10,000,000 until it is completely eliminated for estates over $21,040,000. The 60% bracket is a result of a 5% surtax on amounts over $10,000,000 but less than $21,595,000 at which point the average tax rate on the entire estate averages 55%.

Some states with estate taxes require that the deceased's bank accounts and safety deposit boxes be sealed until tax officials issue a release. In these states, it is definitely not a good idea to store your estate plan in your safety deposit box.

If you live in more than one state, it is important to establish which state is your official domicile (primary place of residence), as this can affect which state governs your estate. If you divide your time fairly equally, it might benefit you to discover which state has more beneficial estate tax laws, and make it your domicile. The state in which you vote and maintain most of your major personal business contacts is usually considered your domicile.

It is important to note that your estate will be able to deduct all or some of any state or foreign taxes owed on property you owned at home or elsewhere and expenses incurred after your death for the funeral, legal and probate fees and any claims successfully made against your estate.

How do I estimate any state or foreign estate taxes that might be due? Every state except the **estate-tax states**—Mississippi, New York, North Carolina, Ohio, and Oklahoma—has abolished state estate taxes, at least in effect. (New York is phasing out its tax.)

In the rest of the states, they either don't have state estate taxes at all, or they take part of the money that you would otherwise pay to the Federal government; it's a matter for accountants and tax preparers, but it doesn't increase the tax bill. These **gap-tax states** technically impose estate taxes and estate tax returns must be filed but the amount is actually equal to the deduction allowed for state taxes, to be taken against federal estate taxes. Therefore the overall amount payable is no greater than if state death taxes were not due. These states collect their share of the tax from the Federal government. Only the estate-tax states impose a tax which is greater than the deduction allowed, thus requiring a greater out-of-pocket payment. Depending on the state and the size of the estate, in these states, the state death taxes can range from 1% to 21%.

If you live in one of the estate tax states mentioned above, contact your state's Internal Revenue Department for details on any exemptions permitted and the tax rates (which increase incrementally as the size of your estate increases).

What if I have property in more than one state or country? If you have property in more than one state or country, **Barry Webster,** an attorney with **Lette, Lette & Partners,** Toronto, Canada, says "Estate tax planning becomes more complicated. Foreign laws may not always recognize the validity or interpretation of a U.S. trust or will, and your estate may become liable for estate taxes which otherwise might have been avoided. Therefore, before finalizing an estate plan, it is crucial that you and your estate planner seek help from professional estate planners located in the same jurisdiction as your property."

Your estate's executor has a few options.

To pay estate taxes, the executor can:

- Pay in cash if it is available.
- Sell some of the property, although often the forced sale of property can bring in considerably smaller proceeds and can be devastating to the estate.
- Borrow money to pay the taxes, if the assets of the estate are not already mortgaged—although lenders may be reluctant to advance funds and interest rates may be prohibitive.
- Request a deferral from the IRS on estate tax payments of up to ten years, if they can show reasonable cause. However, the estate will have to pay interest on the estate tax due, at then current market rates, just as if it were a loan. Fortunately, this interest is deductible from the estate. Sometimes, the IRS demands that a bond, which is not cheap, be posted as security.

When are tax payments due? With few exceptions, the IRS demands that estate taxes must be paid, in cash, nine months from the date of death. Payments cannot be postponed without special approval from the IRS. And delayed payments can result in the IRS seizing the property and selling it in a tax sale.

Are taxes pro-rated between those who will be receiving a portion of my estate? Unless a will or living trust states otherwise, the estate taxes are paid from the estate as a whole before any distributions are made. If you want to vary this by specifying that certain assets be used to pay taxes, you must state that in your will or living trust.

Where will the money come from to pay taxes and fees?

The market value of your property or the available cash can change considerably in the years between the preparation of your estate plan and your death. A plan that might have worked adequately ten years ago, might become completely unfair at your death. Property, other than cash, that you wished to go to a beneficiary may have to be liquidated to pay estate taxes. For this reason, some estate tax planners may recommend obtaining life insurance to cover any estate taxes due. (See pages 34 and 101.)

> THE AVOIDANCE OF TAXES IS THE ONLY INTELLECTUAL PURSUIT THAT CARRIES ANY REWARD.
>
> —John Maynard Keynes

Will my family have to give up our family business?

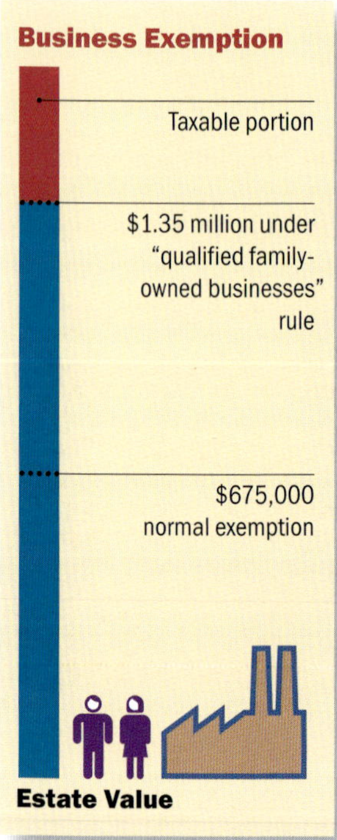

Lack of liquidity can pose difficulties.

Will my family have to give up our family business and their source of income if there is not enough cash to pay estate taxes?
Turning estate assets into cash can be difficult, particularly for closely held family businesses which are the source of a family's income. If forced to sell these properties, which can be difficult to sell at a fair price, families can lose their source of livelihood. For this reason, Congress has passed specific federal estate-tax rules to ease the burden on family business survivors. They include:

- Owners of qualified family-owned businesses can receive exemptions of $1.35 million–twice the current standard exemption of $675,000. There are many technical requirements to receive this extra exemption.
- As long as the business represents at least 35% of the total estate minus its debts and expenses, the business will qualify for an easier payment plan, allowing taxes due–on the business portion of the estate–to be paid over a 14-year period at very low rates.

What if my business is a family corporation?
Many people own all or part of the stock of a corporation, which may not be easy to convert to the cash needed to pay estate taxes—especially if the corporation is not listed on a stock exchange.

Often, however, those corporations have assets that can more readily be converted into cash than does the rest of the estate. Because of this, the Federal government passed Section 303 of the Internal Revenue Code allowing corporations to buy, from an estate, sufficient stock to pay for estate taxes and other death related expenses such as probate, funeral costs and the administration of the estate. If the corporation does not have cash, it can give assets in exchange for the stock which in turn can be sold.

Section 303 provides an easy way to convert non-liquid stock into dollars on the death of a stockholder, but it is a very technical section of the Internal Revenue Code and should not be used without expert advice. There are certain requirements to take advantage of Section 303 and there can be some drawbacks.

What if we own a family farm, ranch or business which is located on valuable land that we don't want to sell? When cities grow, they often encroach on farmland, raising the value of the farm or ranch property far beyond what it is worth as an income-producing farm. If the Federal government were to use the city value for estate tax purposes, it would put almost every farm or ranch family off of their land, forcing them to sell it to pay estate taxes. Therefore, Congress passed a relief provision for special valuation of family farm and ranch properties, as well as for real estate used in other types of family businesses.

This special use valuation tax break can reduce the deceased's federal gross estate by no more than $750,000 (an amount which will be periodically indexed for inflation). To take advantage of special use valuation, there are certain requirements that must be met. Check with your estate planning specialist.

As this section illustrates, there are a variety of ways to make use of different provisions that the IRS has created to ease the burden of estate taxes and their payment. In later chapters, you will find descriptions of estate planning methods that can help to further reduce and even eliminate estate taxes, depending on the size of your estate.

Easy-Payment Plan

With rates as low as 2%, some estate planners recommend that executors try to qualify for the easy-payment plan, even if there is enough cash to pay estate taxes on the family business. The cash could earn a much higher interest rate than the 2% cost of the easy-payment plan and therefore earn additional net income for the beneficiaries of the estate. Your estate does not have to be cash poor to take advantage of the easy-payment plan. However, to be approved for the easy payment plan, you must meet certain qualifications.

There can be many traps for the unwary tax payer for both the easy-payment plan and Section 303. For instance, large gifts that were made in the last three years before death will be brought back into the estate when calculating the 35% requirement, possibly nullifying the use of these plans. Nevertheless, many family businesses have been saved by these plans.

What makes up my estate?

All property that you own wholly or in part makes up your estate and is yours to give away, wholly or in part, although some types of partial ownership can make property harder to give away than others.

Tangible personal property includes such things as your furniture, clothes, jewelry, antiques, books, all kinds of collections, and even your pets.

Liquid assets include your cash, savings accounts, and property that can easily be sold for cash.

Real estate includes any land, such as your home, cabins, or vacation properties.

Your business includes its assets, to the degree that you own them.

Life insurance proceeds are usually included when the Federal government, or the IRS, is determining the value of your **gross estate** for estate taxation purposes. The value of any life insurance policy over which you have any incidences of ownership (which means, among other things, actually owning the policy or the right to change the beneficiary of the policy) is added to the value of your gross estate when you die. But note that the owner of an insurance policy does not have to be the person who is insured. There are ways to remove life insurance from the estate so that the proceeds escape estate taxes (see pages 31 and 100). Fortunately, life insurance proceeds with a third-party beneficiary (other than your estate) do escape probate, at least, and all of its related difficulties and expenses.

Retirement programs with **beneficial interests** are included in your estate for tax purposes. These programs could include individual retirement accounts (IRAs), Keogh plans, pension plans, profit-sharing plans, annuities, tax-sheltered annuities, 401K plans, ESOPs, and any deferred-compensation plans. Although retirement benefits with beneficial interests are included in your taxable estate, they are not included in your probate estate. Therefore, such things as IRAs can serve as a ready source of cash when one spouse dies.

Annuities are considered part of your estate for federal estate tax purposes. The exception to this rule is a straight-life annuity for which all payments end at death. If you paid only a part of the annuity purchase price, then only the related percentage of the annuity is included in your estate, unless it was your employer who paid the other part.

Receivables, money owed to you, become assets of your estate. Your estate would be charged with the responsibility of collecting these amounts and also for payment of estate tax on them. It is also possible to leave in your estate plan the forgiveness of debts that are owed to you. In this event, these debts would not be collected and would be considered a gift.

Debts remaining at your death must be negotiated or paid by your estate and the amounts paid would be **deducted** from your estate before calculating taxes and distributions. Other deductions from your taxable estate would include funeral and legal expenses that are incurred after your death. (This is in contrast to your probate estate for which you may not deduct your debts when calculating it for probate fee purposes.)

Life insurance is insurance that you or someone else takes out on your life, which pays out a specific sum to the named beneficiaries when you die. Life insurance on your life which is owned by someone else is not included in your gross estate.

Gross estate is made up of the fair market value of all of your property, before any debts or liabilities are deducted.

Beneficial interests are produced by investments which continue to provide a benefit to your surviving spouse, children or heirs upon your death.

Annuities are policies in which an insurance company or charity contracts to pay the policy beneficiary (which could be you) a certain cash amount each month or year. You can also name another beneficiary who will continue to receive the periodic payments upon your death.

Consult with a qualified expert if your estate will include retirement plans. **Galen Griepp,** estate planning attorney in Pasadena, California, warns, “There are many subtleties on the subject of retirement assets and many advisors don’t understand them sufficiently.”

If annuity proceeds are paid to a beneficiary, rather than your estate or a trust, the proceeds may not be available to pay the estate taxes the annuity might incur.

How is titled property handled?

Holding title is a legal term which addresses the question of to whom the property really belongs. A title or deed which carries your name proves you own the asset.

Divorced? If you are single, property ownership can be very straightforward. There are people who think they are single after a divorce, but they discover they are not. Be sure you have the paperwork you need to prove that you are legally divorced.

Titled property, to the extent you personally hold title to it, also becomes part of your estate.

How you **hold title** to property determines how much of its value is part of your estate. How you hold title to your assets is very important for estate planning purposes, as it may determine how assets pass to your beneficiaries, how assets are taxed, and even whether the probate process can be avoided. Not everyone knows how they hold title to all of their property, and sometimes the form of title is not optimum for estate planning purposes. The good news is that the title to property can often be changed to give you greater control over your estate, reduce your estate tax burden, avoid probate and make sure that you are able to pass your property along exactly as you want to.

What does it mean when I own property in fee simple? Fee simple is an old fashioned term that means that you and you alone own the whole thing. Most real estate held by unmarried people is held in fee simple. Since this is an old term that is not used very often any more, your title is most likely to read, Jane Doe, an unmarried woman or Jane Doe, a married woman, as her sole and separate property. If you are married but want to hold the property in fee simple, you must specify it on the title so that your spouse is not automatically assumed to be a co-owner according to state laws. Married people are entitled to own separate property, either by agreement with their partners, or because they received the property as an inheritance, gift or legal settlement while married, or they owned it before the marriage. When you own something in fee simple, and the evidence of ownership, the title, is clear, you can sell it, trade it, give it away or leave it to whom you choose upon your death. If you think you own something in fee simple and your title indicates differently, you must undertake to correct it with the help of a professional.

What does owning property in joint tenancy mean? Joint tenancy with right of survivorship (JTWROS) is a form of ownership in which two or more individuals each own 100% of the same asset or piece of property. For instance if there were two owners, they would not own 50% each, but they would both own 100%. The right of survivorship feature also means that the asset is owned only by the living owners listed on the title. If you were to die, your portion of the ownership in the property would not become a part of your estate to be passed onto your beneficiaries named in your will or trust, but would be owned wholly by the surviving joint tenants on the title.

Using joint tenancy has become a popular method for avoiding the probate process, but has complications you should be aware of:

- Your heirs or beneficiaries, other than those joint owners listed on the title, would not have any rights to the property—meanwhile the value of your interest in the property is still included in your gross estate for estate tax purposes. Aside from choosing who to become joint tenants with, you have no control over who the property goes to upon your death.
- If one of the owners is declared legally incompetent, joint accounts can be frozen by law until the courts have appointed a conservator.
- If all people listed on the title were to die at the same time, there would be separate probate proceedings required for each person listed.
- If you are a joint tenant with your spouse, one half of the property would be included in the estate of the first to die, for taxation purposes and all of the property would be included in the estate of the last spouse to die, resulting in potentially heavy taxation.
- Without special planning, the last living owner of a jointly-held asset would have to include the full value of the property in his or her estate, even though he or she was originally only part owner of the property.
- Only the heirs or beneficiaries named by the last living owner would inherit the property, and they would inherit the entire property.

Sometimes more than one name appears on a title but the type of ownership is not specified. The nature of the ownership varies from state to state—in some you are automatically tenants in common, in others, you are joint tenants, depending on the laws of your state. Don't assume anything—find out from your advisors which kind of ownership is the default.

THE COMFORTABLE ESTATE OF WIDOWHOOD IS THE ONLY HOPE THAT KEEPS UP A WIFE'S SPIRITS.

—JOHN GAY

Partitioning requires that a court take an asset and make it an actual, physical division, based on each tenant's percentage of ownership.

Undivided interest means that the owners do not own any particular part of the property.

There are two potential disadvantages to tenancy in common ownership. First, you do not know which part of the property you own, and to determine this would require legal partitioning by the courts. Second, when a new tenant has purchased or inherited a partial interest, the remaining tenants may not get along with them.

- Creditors for any one person on the title can go after the entire property to settle a claim.
- While you can give away or sell your joint tenancy, it might be difficult to do so, unless the purchaser is willing to accept the limitations of joint tenancy. To separate your portion, to make it more attractive to a buyer, you would have to have a judge legally **partition** the property, creating either separate shares or a tenancy in common.

What does it mean when I own property as a tenant in common? With property you own with others as a tenant in common, each tenant owns a partial but **undivided interest** in the property. Usually, although not always, the tenants in common own equal shares of the property. For instance, if there are two tenants, each owns half, or if there are three tenants, each owns one third of the property. To own unequal shares of the property, there must be a written agreement to that effect. Otherwise, equal ownership is assumed. Each tenant owns the property in common with the other tenants and each tenant is free to sell, give, or upon death, leave his or her share of the property to whomever they choose, to be established in their estate plans. In the absence of an estate plan, your portion would be included in your estate both for estate tax and probate fee purposes and would go to your heirs according to local intestate laws. There is no limit as to how many tenants in common there can be.

What does it mean when I own property as tenancy by the entirety? This is a special form of joint ownership between spouses and is available in only a limited number of states. Similar to joint tenancy, it has a right of survivorship feature which means that upon the death of the first spouse, the survivor automatically owns the entire asset. Subsequently it avoids probate at the first death. Unlike joint tenancy, this form of title provides protection from creditors to married couples. Property held in the entirety is not generally available to the individual creditors of the husband or the wife, should creditors win a claim against them.

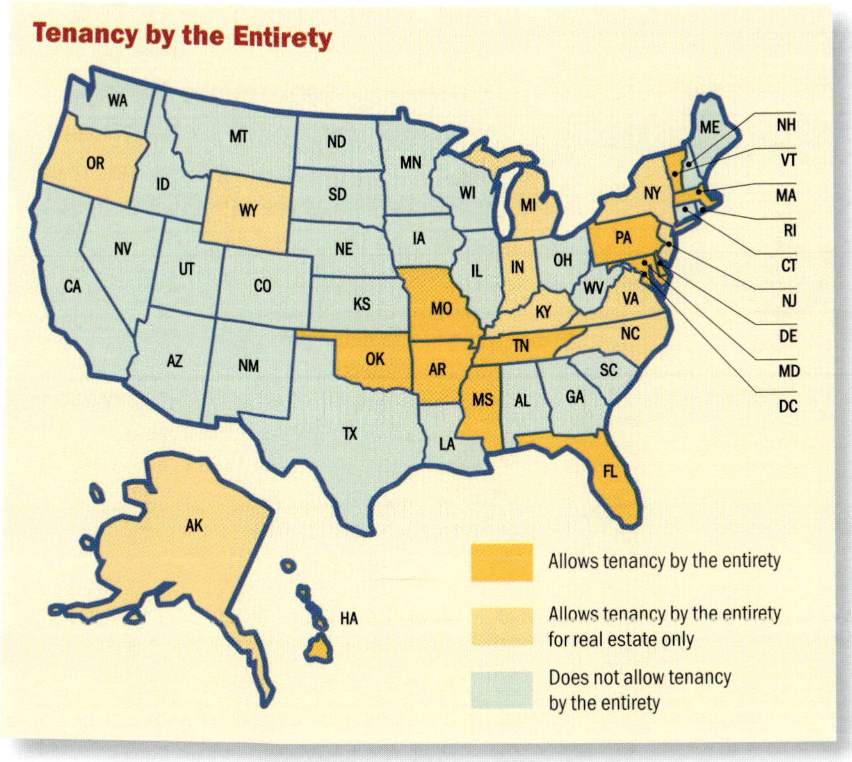

However, if both husband and wife are liable on the same debt, their tenancy by the entirety property could be available to their mutual creditor.

What if there are no documents to prove ownership of our property? When there is no document of ownership for an item, its status must be determined by looking at the history of the property or possession. How was it obtained? Who paid for it? Was it a gift or a loan? Is there any history which might show that the property actually belongs to two or more people together, to an ex-spouse, or even to a current spouse as his or her separate (exclusive) property? Was the property properly transferred to you in the first place? However you go about establishing ownership, in the case of more valuable property, legally establishing ownership is a crucial aspect of estate planning.

How does marriage affect ownership of property?

Prenuptial agreements are agreements made between a husband and wife, before they are married, to delineate property ownership of the property they owned individually before the marriage and any property acquired by them during the marriage.

The ownership laws of the state in which you live or own property determine how marital property is handled.

What are marital property ownership laws?

If you are married, it is important that you understand the marital property laws of the state you live in and in any state in which you own property. No matter where you live, the laws of the state in which the property is located are the ownership laws that are applicable to that property, although a valid **prenuptial agreement** can override the normal marital property presumptions. States can be broadly divided into two types—community property states and common law property states.

Common Law vs. Community Property States

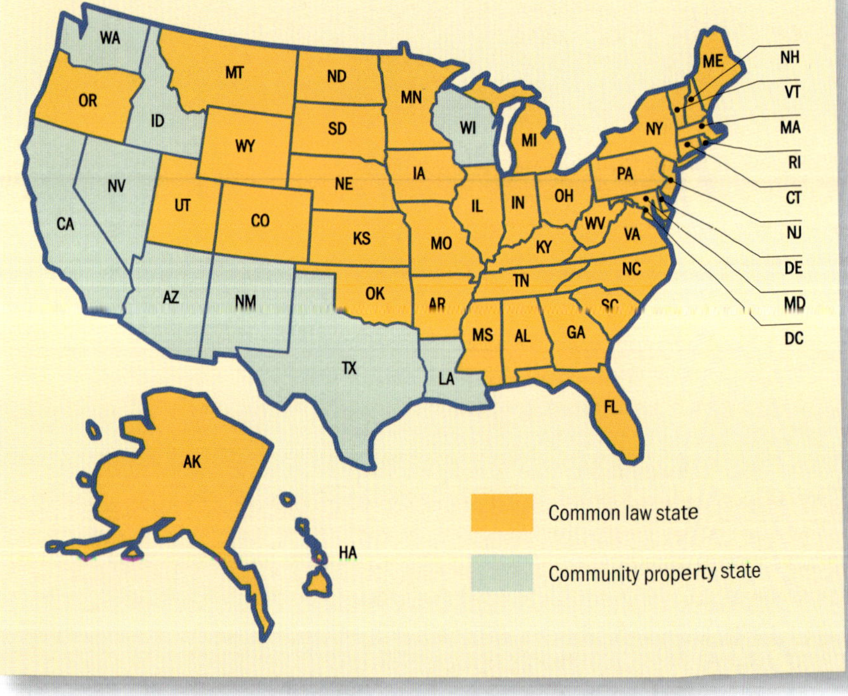

What's the difference between community property and common law ownership laws?

The conceptual foundation for the community property form of ownership is that a marriage relationship takes on a unique form that is different from any other relationship or agreement. In a community property state, the marriage or community actually exists as a separate entity, created by two individuals who have entered into a legal marriage.

Common law principles are derived from English law, where in feudal times the husband owned all marital property and a wife had few property ownership rights and was unable to leave property in her will. Still today, in common law states, the spouse who earns money or acquires property owns it solely and separately unless he or she transfers it into shared ownership.

Community Property Law

Community property law is derived from the ancient marriage laws of some European peoples. Only nine maverick states are community property law states, as allowed by the tenth amendment to the U.S. Constitution. As a result, the Federal government had to structure estate and gift taxes so that they would fairly apply to all citizens of all states.

Community property and common law ownership laws are distinctly different and come from different legal traditions.

What if I live in a community property state?

All of your separate property, plus one-half of your community property, make up your estate.

What is community property? The assumptions attached to this concept are that everything earned or acquired by the married couple should be viewed as belonging to the marriage or community, and is therefore owned equally by the partners, no matter whose name is on the title. Community property generally includes:

- All employment income received by either spouse during the course of the marriage;
- All property acquired with that employment income;
- All property which had been separate property but is transformed into community property through a gift to the community (by, for example, changing the deed of a piece of property); or
- Commingling separate property with community property such that it is hard to identify one from the other (putting money from both into one bank account, for instance).

What is separate property? In community property states, separate property is property owned entirely by only one spouse. Property owned by one spouse before the marriage remains separate after the marriage as long as it is kept legally separate. Also, any inheritances left to just one spouse by will or living trust are his or her separate property. If, however, that separate property is sold and the proceeds commingled with other marriage partnership activities and investments, it generally becomes a part of a community partnership's holdings. Separate property can also be given from one spouse to another as a gift. It is also possible to maintain income as separate property in all community states except Washington. This is only the case, however, if both partners sign a written agreement to do so and then actually keep the income separate. In the event that separate property generates income, that income is also considered separate property in California, Arizona, Nevada, New Mexico and Washington. In Texas and Idaho, income from separate property is community property. Wisconsin statutes are still being refined and interpreted. You should consult with a Wisconsin professional if you think this topic is relevant to you.

WHAT'S MINE IS MINE, AND HALF OF WHAT'S OURS IS MINE.

—Galen Griepp, Griepp and McRee

How is my estate affected in community property states? In community property states, what you own is all of your separate property and one half of community property. Together this makes up your estate. Community property, as a form of ownership, confers different powers on the owners than does joint tenancy, which confers no power on the owner when it comes to passing property upon death. With community property, there are no restrictions on how each spouse can give away his or her half of community property on their death. Neither is required to leave their share to the surviving spouse, although many choose to. It is important to note, however, that while the marriage may still be legally intact, once a couple permanently separates, in most community

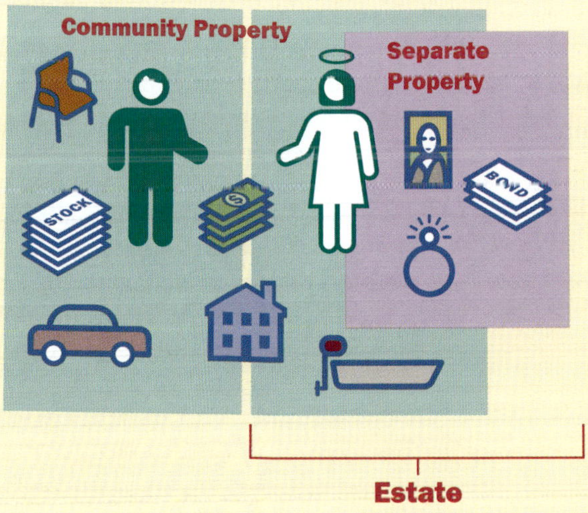

In community property states, your estate is all your separate property and one-half of community property.

property states their subsequent income and acquisitions become their own separate property, as do the debts they incur, unless there is some other agreement contrary to this.

What if I don't know which property is separate and which is community? In many cases, when property has been sold and reinvested, or held over a long period of years, or acquired under uncertain circumstances, it is difficult to determine whether property is community or separate. If there is any doubt as to classification, the law usually favors community property status. Separate property can be sold and the proceeds invested in another asset and that asset can be considered separate if the source of funds can be directly traced back to proceeds from the sale of the original separate property. If, however, in the process of selling a property and buying another, the proceeds went into a joint bank account and commingled with joint funds, the asset will lose its classification as separate property. In the case of appreciated property, when the separate property goes up in value, this appreciation is also separate. However, in some cases, a home, for example, is cared for, maintained and improved by both spouses during a marriage, even though the title indicates separate property. The result can be that the property is partially separate and partially community. Calculating the percentages can be quite difficult. The easiest solution is for both spouses to come to an amicable and fair agreement and put it in writing.

In the case of a privately owned business, it can be even more difficult. If both spouses work in the business, it would be sensible to agree it is community property or establish a separate legal entity (a partnership or corporation) for the business. If only one spouse works in the business, resolving ownership can be much more difficult.

Another gray area is in the event that one spouse has received monetary recovery for personal injuries. Generally, this is considered

The name or names on the title to a property do not necessarily determine its status as community or separate property.

Family Business

Joint ownership of a business should be documented as community property or you should establish a separate legal entity for the business.

separate property but not always. In some community property states, this money is treated as community property while the injured spouse is alive and as separate property upon his or her death. If the injury is caused by the other spouse, it can become even more complicated. There are no easy answers for this type of property.

If spouses plan to leave all or most of their property to each other or in a way that the other approves of, determining the character of the property is not crucial. However, if you and your spouse find any conflict over ownership, you should find a way to work it out as it will affect your estate planning. If necessary, it is better to resolve it now with the help of a professional—a mediator, a counselor, or a lawyer—than to let the confusion remain. A nasty court fight could ensue if one spouse dies and has tried to leave property that the other spouse doesn't believe he or she owns. A written **Marital Property Agreement** that describes how they intend to own their property, with the intention of correcting any misconceptions that the title or state laws might create, can be signed by both spouses to ensure a peaceful handling of property.

IF WE DO NOT CHOOSE TO PLAN, THEN WE CHOOSE TO HAVE OTHERS PLAN FOR US.

—Richard I. Winword

You CAN Take it With You

Most states consider money received for personal injury to be community property while the injured spouse is still alive but as separate property upon his or her death.

What if I live in a common law state?

Generally, what you earn, purchase with your income, or hold title to is part of your estate.

What is common law property? In common law states, there is no rule that property acquired during a marriage is owned by both spouses. But, whether you are married or not, in common law states, you separately own everything that was purchased with your income or property. If joint income is used, then the ownership is considered shared and usually considered a tenancy in common (see page 38). You also separately own everything legally held in just your name—that is, property for which you have a title slip, deed or some other legal ownership document. Whose name is on the title determines the legal ownership. For instance, if you earn the money but you put a new house in both your and your spouse's names, you both own it. Or if your spouse earns the income but you take title in your name alone, then you own it. It is usually true, however, that in a divorce, the courts according to an **equitable distribution law** will not endorse an obvious injustice and may attempt to straighten matters out.

Do family members have any protection in common law states? To protect a spouse from being left with nothing and entirely disinherited after his or her spouse's death, common law states give a surviving spouse a certain percentage of the deceased's estate. In most common law states, the surviving spouse is entitled to a minimum of one-third of the property left by the other, and in some states they are entitled to one-half. The exact amount is often determined by whether or not there are dependent children. In some states, only the property left via the will—or that which goes through probate—is included in the calculation. In other states, all the property transferred, whether by will, living trust, or by other means such as joint tenancy, is included in determining the percentage received. Therefore, those assets left in such a way as to avoid probate are not left out of the equation.

Gray Areas

Wherever there are gray areas, there are potential court battles, so it benefits everybody if all marital property ownership questions are handled amicably and while both spouses are still alive and together.

Equitable distribution laws in most common law property states give the courts the power to divide marital property fairly—which is often equally, no matter what the title, deed, or ownership documents say.

Spousal Inheritance Rights

If the deceased spouse leaves nothing to the surviving spouse, or less than his or her minimum **statutory share** (the share a person is entitled to according to state law), in most states, the surviving spouse has a choice of either taking what the will or other transfer document provides or rejecting the gift and instead taking the minimum share allowed by state law. This is called taking against the will.

What if I move to a state with different ownership laws?

Have your estate plan reviewed by an attorney in your new state.

What happens if we move from a common law state to a community property state or vice versa? When changing between states which have different types of ownership laws, there can be a problem. And some estate planning devices do better than others at crossing state lines. If, however, both spouses plan to leave most or all of their estate to each other anyway, this will pose less of a problem, although certain types of estate planning devices—certain kinds of wills, for instance—may not be accepted at all in some states.

How do we assess our property when moving from a common law state to a community property state? California and Idaho, both community property states, treat the earlier acquired property as if it had been acquired in a community property state. For instance, if one spouse purchased a car in her name only in New York and then moved it to California, it would be deemed community property, according to California statute. The legal name for this type of property is **quasi-community property.** However, for estate purposes, the other community property states (Arizona, Louisiana, Nevada, New Mexico, Texas, Washington and Wisconsin) go by the rules of the state in which the property was acquired. (Texas and Arizona recognize quasi-community property only for the purposes of divorce.)

How do we assess our property when moving from a community property state to a common law state? The common law property states generally recognize that each spouse retains interest in the property accumulated in the marriage while they still lived in a community property state. But, the courts have not been consistent in dealing with property that is in only one spouse's name. Laws of their new state of residence usually govern for all income and new property acquired after the move.

If you move from one state to another, you should determine whether or not you and your spouse need to make changes in ownership papers to reflect your true intentions of ownership.

IF ANYTHING IS CERTAIN, IT IS THAT CHANGE IS CERTAIN. THE WORLD WE ARE PLANNING FOR TODAY WILL NOT EXIST IN THIS FORM TOMORROW.

—Phillip Crosby

What do I need to know about wills?

When the term estate planning is used, most people think of writing a will. Similarly, many people who have prepared a will believe that they have an estate plan. While most estate planners say that this is only one step in the right direction, wills have an important role to play.

A will is a **revocable document** that sets out how you, the **testator** or **testatrix** (if female), wish to transfer your property upon your death. Wills usually designate an executor—the person who will carry out your instructions. And if you have dependents, wills should also specify who their guardians and the guardians of their property should be. Usually one guardian does both; however, it is possible to split these tasks.

Otherwise, all wills are unique, depending on what property you own, how you want it distributed, and so on. While wills are not normally made public until your death, after your death, they become public documents which must be filed with the local courts and the contents are made part of the public record. Everyone and anyone can access the contents of the will as well as data on all your assets and debts, and the proceedings disposing of them.

The people named to receive bequests (gifts from you) in your will are called beneficiaries. This is in contrast to heirs, which is the term used to describe people who would inherit your estate, as determined by state law, should you leave no will or will substitute. In your will, you can leave your property to as many or as few people or organizations as you choose, although, as discussed in the section on common law states (see page 40), the laws will protect the rights of spouses, no matter what your will provides.

Where you are domiciled or have your domicile (the state in which you have your primary residence) affects your will in a number of ways. Not only do different states have different rules that govern the rights of family members, they also have different **will execution** requirements. And in addition to federal estate taxes, some states also charge state death taxes and inheritance taxes—taxes that the beneficiary pays along with their income taxes on the value of the property they receive from you (see page 26).

When writing a will, you must think ahead as much as possible. You should ask yourself the following questions:

- Who should receive a bequest in the event that the beneficiary or charity you have named dies before you do? Perhaps the estate or heirs of the deceased beneficiary would be good candidates.
- What if, at your death, you no longer own some of the property you have left in your will to a beneficiary but you want that beneficiary to receive something? Instead of leaving a **specific bequest** which you might not still own at the time of your death, you might want to consider leaving the cash value of that specific bequest instead, or a **residuary bequest.**

By addressing these types of possibilities in the will itself, you do not have to rewrite or make changes to your will every time something pertaining to it changes. A lawyer can help to write a will that covers all contingencies.

Revocable document is one you can cancel at any time.

Testator/testatrix is the person who makes the will. The testator/testatrix must be an adult and must be of sound mind at the time of signing a will, in order for the will to be considered valid. This is called testamentary capacity. Your physical condition is irrelevant, as long as you can understand what you are doing. That is why wills usually contain the phrase "being of sound mind."

Will execution is the process of signing, witnessing, and notarizing your will.

Specific bequest is a specific gift to a beneficiary which could be a piece of property, such as jewelry or real estate.

Residuary bequest is a percentage of the remainder of your estate, once specific bequests have been made.

Wills do not avoid probate. Many people erroneously believe that they can avoid probate by writing a will. While there are probate-avoiding estate plan vehicles, a will is not one of them. Over 90% of wills end up in probate court.

What can a will do for me?

A will is good, but if you die before making a more complete estate plan, your heirs and your estate may pay a price.

With a will, you can...

- Achieve minimum estate planning at somewhat lower cost and less paperwork than other estate planning devices.
- Name a guardian for your children and their property, and leave property for them in a testamentary trust (see page 61).
- Appoint an executor for your estate.
- Give your property to persons or organizations of your choosing, whether or not they would otherwise be legal heirs.
- Disinherit or exclude anyone you wish to, within the limits of state laws on family rights (see page 116).
- Provide a back up for an estate plan, which has something other than a will as the primary transfer device, to cover anything that is overlooked or not included.

Parts of a Will

1. Your name and address.
2. A brief description of your assets.
3. Names of spouse, children and other beneficiaries, such as charities, friends or relatives.
4. Alternate beneficiaries, in case a beneficiary dies before you do.
5. Specific gifts, such as a car or your home.
6. Any establishment of testamentary trusts and the designation of a trustee (see page 61).
7. Any cancellation of debts as a gift.
8. Name of the executor to manage the estate.
9. Name of a guardian(s) for minor children and their property.
10. Name of an alternate guardian, in the event your first choice is unwilling or unable to act.
11. Your signature.
12. Witnesses' signatures.
13. The signature and stamp of a notary public (in some states).

What can a will not do for me?

With a will, you cannot...

- Avoid probate. As required by law, most wills must be probated. Sometimes, when passing property from one spouse to another, a petition procedure can be used to bypass probate. In the case of very tiny estates, in some states there can be shortened or summary probate which is not as long and drawn out.
- Maintain privacy. Once filed with probate court, your will becomes a public document, available for anyone to see.
- Protect your instructions from being challenged in court. Anyone can know the contents of your will, which makes it easier to contest it.
- Demand that your executor hire a specific attorney to handle your will's probate, although you can informally state a preference.
- Try to encourage or discourage certain kinds of behavior in your beneficiaries. If your beneficiary is a minor, the courts will decide what conditions are appropriate for their receipt of their inheritance. But you cannot make your bequest dependent upon such criteria as your beneficiaries' marriage, divorce or religious practices in a will. Although you can make it contingent upon other behavior, such as going to college—this type of limitation has its drawbacks as certain questions can arise, such as: How soon must your beneficiary go to college? What happens to the gift in the meantime? What if he or she applies in earnest but doesn't get accepted? What if he or she attends school but doesn't study or attend classes? Anytime you wish to impose conditions on a gift, you must leave someone in charge to ensure that the conditions are met. But, to do so requires a different vehicle—a trust (see page 60).

The History of Wills

Most of the laws of wills today are very old and come from the English tradition. Centuries ago, common folk were unable to leave their property to their loved ones. Upon their death, most of their property passed (escheated) to royalty. Then, in 1540, English Parliament made some very progressive changes and created the Statute of Wills. It allowed the common people the right, with certain rules and regulations, to pass all of their property to others on their death. The rules adopted were very complicated, and became more so as different questions and issues arose over time.

> THE MAN WHO WAITS TO MAKE AN ENTIRELY REASONABLE WILL, DIES INTESTATE.
>
> —Bernard Shaw

What property can I dispose of with my will?

In some states, you may set up bank accounts, bonds, and certificates of deposits (CDs) as payable on death to whomever you choose. These states include the following: Alabama, Alaska, Arizona, California, Colorado, Florida, Hawaii, Idaho, Maine, Michigan, Minnesota, Montana, Nebraska, New Jersey, New Mexico, North Dakota, South Carolina, Texas and Utah.

Always name adults or a trust as your beneficiary on a POD account and you will avoid probate. When minors receive an inheritance without a trust set up to manage it, the bequest must go through probate and then must be overseen by the courts until the child reaches the age of majority—18 or 21, depending on the state.

Designated beneficiary is the person(s) or trust you specify should receive the proceeds of your life insurance or your retirement plans. The name of the beneficiary is written right on the form or policy.

Your will can include all of your property except...

- Property that you own in joint ownership with right of survivorship (JTRWOS) or tenancy by the entirety (TE) with others (see page 37). You can, however, make provisions in your will for your share of the property to go to whomever you choose, should you be the last living joint tenant.
- Property that is owned by a living trust (see page 61).
- Bank accounts or E, EE, or H United States bonds, which are payable on death (POD) accounts (also known as bank account trusts [BAT] or Totten Trusts. Totten means death in German.)
- Property that you have previously contracted to sell or give away or that has contractual controls or limits imposed upon it.
- Property that you don't legally own at your death. Most of us buy and sell (or give away) property and investments throughout our adult lives. Unless a will is regularly and specifically updated, it may leave property which you no longer own at the time of death.
- The benefits of a life insurance policy which have **designated beneficiaries** other than your estate. Cash from life insurance policies with your estate named as the designated beneficiary can be included in your will.
- Pension or retirement plans for which you have designated a beneficiary.

The assets listed above will pass outside of your will, which means that they also pass outside of probate (see page 16). They are referred to as non-probate assets and are not affected by the provisions of your will.

Sometimes you can dispose of another person's property in your own will—property for which you have been granted power of appointment. This means someone left you the use of property during your lifetime and the authority to dispose of it on your subsequent death.

To write a will...

- You must be of legal age.
- You must be of sound mind and memory. This means that you know what you are doing, know what property you own, and know who you are leaving the property to. A will-maker has to be much more than just absent-minded or forgetful to be deemed not of sound mind. A court assumes that the writer was of sound mind, unless someone challenges it in a court.
- The wording in the will must indicate that you really intend the document to be your will—your final say on the disposition of your property.
- The will must be voluntarily signed by you or someone else who you have authorized to do so—in the event of illness, accident or illiteracy. (Do not do this unless you have a very thorough understanding of the relevant laws of your state.)
- All states have their own standards for formal wills. While some states do allow oral wills and un-witnessed wills in some circumstances, wills usually must be signed and witnessed by at least two adults who are aware of what it is they are witnessing and are competent to testify in court, should the need arise. In most states the witnesses cannot be beneficiaries of the will.
- All wills must be executed a certain way—complying with certain technical requirements as set forth in your state's laws. For example, some states require a will to include a statement at the end which says that it is your will; the date and place of signing; the fact that you signed it in the presence of the witnesses; and the fact that the witnesses also signed both in your presence and in each others' presence.
- Most states will allow what are called self-proving affidavits to create a self-proving will, which eliminates the necessity of having witnesses testify after your death that they witnessed the signing of your will. In some states, the witnesses are required to testify and in the event of their death or if they are unavailable, the courts will seek someone who can verify the missing witnesses' signature.
- A will is not required to be recorded or filed with any government agency, although in some states it is possible to do so.

What are the requirements for writing a will?

To make a will, in most states you must be at least 18 years of age. In Georgia it is 14, in Louisiana it is 16, 21 in New Jersey. In most states, if you are married or plan to be married, you may make a will at an earlier age. Indiana makes a similar exception for a person in the Armed Forces and the Merchant Marines.

Laws Governing the Making of a Will

Usually, a will is valid in any state in the United States, provided it was valid in the state in which you were domiciled when the will was made. If you move, you should have your will reviewed by an attorney in your new state to see whether your will is going to be read the way you intended it to be. A new will may be necessary.

Legally you are not required to use a lawyer or other professional to write a will. As long as the will meets the legal requirements of your state, it is valid. Nevertheless, wills are usually prepared by a lawyer, and signed in the presence of a lawyer, witnesses and sometimes a notary. If you have an estate that is complicated by a business that you own or some other factor, if you think that some unhappy relative might challenge the will, or if your estate is substantial, it is especially advisable that you use a lawyer.

Are there different types of wills?

Wills vary by who is making the will and what form the will is in.

A typed witnessed will is a conventional will—the kind familiar to courts—and is what most people speak of when they refer to a will.

A statutory will or the mystic will is a preprinted, fill-in-the-blanks, check-the-boxes form and is valid only in a few states including California, Wisconsin and Maine. In theory, these wills are reliable, inexpensive, and easy to complete. In reality, however, many consider them so limited as to be of little use. These forms cannot legally be changed so they cannot be adapted to your own personal situation.

A simple will provides only for an outright distribution of assets for an uncomplicated estate.

A joint will is a typed document, which might constitute a contract, that covers both a husband and a wife, or any two people. Each leaves everything to the other when the first dies, and then the will goes on to specify what happens to the property when the second one dies. In effect, a joint will prevents the second person from changing his or her mind about what happens to the first person's property. Joint wills normally tie up property for years, pending the second person's death. It can be uncertain if the survivor can revoke any part of the will and this can often result in litigation. This type of will is not often recommended as other estate planning can accomplish much the same effect without the same drawbacks.

A pour-over will is a will that you use in conjunction with a living trust (see page 61). At your death, it transfers over to the trust any property that had not yet been put into the name of the trust.

Now that I have a will, what do I do with it?

Sign only one original will. If you sign duplicates and one duplicate original is destroyed, the state law may request that they all be destroyed. You can distribute unsigned copies; however, although this could cause confusion later if you make subsequent wills.

Store your will in a safe place where it can be easily found by others and tell your family, verbally and in writing, where they can find it. Many attorneys recommend leaving your will with them in a fire-proof vault, or you may choose to leave a copy with your attorney with a note on it stating the location of the original. It may or may not be a good idea to store your will in your safety deposit box. If your state has a death tax, the box may be sealed until the tax examiner gets around to inspecting its contents, thus holding up the entire proceeding.

Be sure that anyone who receives unsigned copies of your will also receives unsigned copies of any codicils or amendments (see page 56), and that the original codicils are stored with the original will.

A holographic or handwritten will must be written, dated and signed entirely in the handwriting of the person making the will. Holographic wills are recognized in about 25 states. They need not be witnessed. Some attorneys recommend holographic wills as a good interim measure when there is no money to pay a lawyer. Although some are concerned that the courts will view this type of will as less reliable, there are others who view it favorably because the writer was able to string together coherent sentences and thoughts versus just signing something a lawyer typed up. While caution is appropriate, this type of will does have a purpose to serve.

A Good Start...

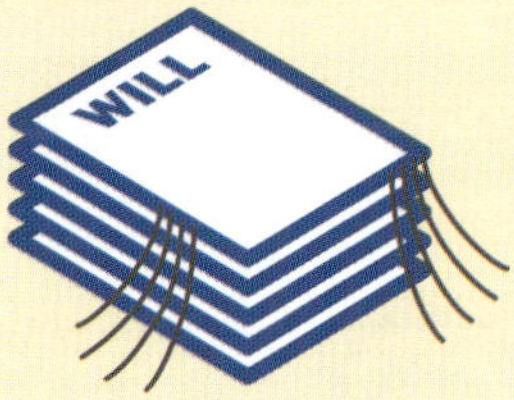

More than 85% of Americans with a will had the help of a lawyer in preparing it, but a large majority of wills are not regularly updated.

A nuncupative or oral will is valid in only a minority of states. Although some states are much stricter, they are generally valid in special circumstances, where, for example, the will-maker is facing sudden and imminent death. In California, for instance, oral wills are accepted only when given by someone serving in the Armed Forces, just before death, for personal property only and totaling less than $1,000. It is therefore not wise to put off making a will, thinking that you can always, on your deathbed, just tell someone what you what want to give to whom.

A contract to make a will is a contract which commits the signer to leave certain property to the other party in the contract and is considered valid. These contracts even take precedence over subsequent wills. These types of contracts usually take place when someone has provided some sort of service—such as live-in nursing—in return for the property cited in the contract. These contracts are not considered desirable as they tie up your property so that you can't ever change your will. A better alternative would be to establish a trust for these situations.

A WILL IS A LEGAL DEVICE TO GET PEOPLE TO EXECUTE THE WISHES OF THE DEAD MORE FAITHFULLY THAN THE WISHES OF THE LIVING.

—Anonymous

How do I update or revoke my will?

A codicil is an amendment to a will. It is used to make minor changes such as changes of individual bequests or the person named as the executor.

Sometimes divorce results in the automatic cancellation of a will. Moral—If you get divorced, redo your will.

When you revoke a later will, it does not revive an earlier will, unless the terms of the revocation state that intention, or unless the first will is republished—that is dated, signed and witnessed again.

Your will will be considered revoked in most states if spouses or children are not mentioned. Due to their statutory share rights (see page 50), if you fail to mention them in your will—that is by expressly disinheriting them—the court will view your will as revoked as far as the unmentioned family members are concerned. However, other provisions will stand.

If you need to make changes, you can amend your will or revoke it entirely and make a new will.

How do I make updates to my will? Over the course of your lifetime, you will probably have to update your will several times. Changes in your marital status, the birth of child, a move to a new state or a substantial change in who you choose as beneficiaries all warrant an update. Simple changes to your will can be made by means of a **codicil** or amendment. Although codicils need to be drafted with all of the same legal formalities (signatures, witnesses etc.) as a written will, they are usually used for minor matters.

In a codicil, you would make reference to your will. You could title it the First, Second, etc., Codicil of the Will of (your name) dated (the date of the will). Then you would revoke any clauses that you wish to change and add any new clause(s), or you can simply add a new provision. Once a codicil is completed, it should be stored with the original will. If you desire to make substantial changes, it is better to revoke your will and draft a new one.

How do I revoke my will? To revoke a will, you must do so by a deliberate act through a specific written statement. In many states you can also revoke your will by burning, tearing, concealing, defacing, obliterating or destroying it. This can be legally done by someone other than yourself, at your instruction. The problem with only destroying a will is that, if you have distributed copies of the will, it could become a source of controversy after your death, especially if not everyone knew you intended to destroy it. For this reason, the written statement, in addition—if you wish to physically destroy the will—is the only way to make your intentions clear.

How is my will executed after I die?

Your executor goes to work.

1
Your executor locates your will.

2
The executor hires an attorney for the probate proceedings.

3
The attorney handles the probate court proceedings.

4
The probate court officially appoints the executor, issuing letters of administration— the legal authority to conduct the estate's business.

5
The probate court officially appoints the persons named in your will to be legal guardians of any dependents and their property.

6
The executor handles any problems, pays debts, including taxes, and takes on such tasks as notifying Social Security and other agencies, canceling credit cards, magazine subscriptions, etc.

7
Money or property left to a trust or trusts created in your will is distributed to the designated trustee.

8
Once probate is finished, the remaining property is distributed as your will instructs.

Do I need more than a will?

Estate planning specialists recommend that a will is only a part of an overall estate plan.

It is very common for people to confuse will making with estate planning and having a will with having an estate plan.

Pros of Having a Will

1. Name the recipients of property not already disposed of by other means, however you choose.
2. Disinherit anyone you choose (within state family estate laws).
3. Choose who will manage your estate.
4. Choose who will be the guardian of your dependents and their property.
5. Provide a back up for property not accounted for in other estate planning vehicles
6. Establish at least a portion of your estate plan relatively quickly and inexpensively.
7. Establish a testamentary trust for the benefit of children and other dependents and to choose the trustee.
8. Establish bypass trusts to better utilize estate tax exemptions and to choose the trustee.

Cons of Having a Will

1. Must go through the probate process.
2. Is made public, revealing your financial and family affairs.
3. Is not effective until you are dead—it does not provide any methods for managing your estate while you are alive.
4. May not control all of your property.
5. Does not provide for your care or management of your property if you should become mentally or physically incapacitated.
6. Is not always read as you intended, especially if you move from state to state or own property in more than one state.
7. Is open to challenge—with second and third marriages producing two of more sets of children, this is occurring more frequently.
8. Requires secure storage and can disappear, in which case your state's intestate laws take over.
9. Can be difficult to change, since the rules applying to wills also apply to codicils. An improperly prepared codicil can be ignored by probate court.

Given the limitations of a will and the challenge that probate offers, many estate planning specialists recommend that a will be only a small part of an overall estate plan.

Jacqueline Kennedy Onassis went to great lengths during her lifetime to maintain privacy. Ironically, she chose to dispose of her estate by means of a will, exposing her financial affairs to the public.

What are trusts?

Trusts allow people to transfer ownership of their property to others, either during their lifetime, or after death. Trusts also make it possible for people to make gifts but still exert some pre-arranged control over the disposition of the gifts in the trust—to truly make gifts with strings attached.

Trusts allow people to give what they have to whom they want, when they want and in the manner that they want. Trusts can also be used to help reduce taxes, attorneys fees and probate costs. Trusts are designed to accomplish a wide variety of estate planning objectives. Most attorneys will consider an assortment of trust instruments to meet the needs of their clients.

Think of a trust as an empty container into which you can place assets.

A trust is created by a **trust maker** through the creation of a **trust document.** Trusts can sometimes be made by more than one person. When there is more than one, they are called joint makers or co-makers.

The written trust document (or instrument) contains all the terms and provisions of the trust. It must set forth a statement of purpose and instructions issued by the trust maker as to the details of the disposition of the **trust property.** A **trustee** is named to be in charge of carrying out the trust maker's instructions. The trust must also spell out the amount of control the trustee has to distribute funds and invade the principal or main asset of the trust, as well as any restrictions on distribution of funds or their use. To be effective, all trusts must be in writing and signed by the trust maker. A single trust document can contain any number of separate trusts.

Trusts can be established to meet just about any objective you would like that does not break the law or go against public policy. They can be created for the benefit of the trust maker and/or the benefit of others. Those who receive the benefit are called beneficiaries and there can be as many beneficiaries as desired. The beneficiaries who first benefit from the trust are called the primary beneficiaries. If the primary beneficiaries die or become disqualified according to the instructions given to the trustee, the property will then go to others, called the contingent beneficiaries.

Trusts cannot last indefinitely (no longer than 121 years) unless the beneficiary is a legally established charity. So there is some limit to how long you can maintain control over the assets you leave your beneficiaries.

While there are many different kinds of trusts, there are two primary categories—death trusts, which are called **testamentary trusts,** and **living trusts,** which are also known as inter vivos trusts.

Trust makers are also called trustors, settlors, donors, creators or grantors.

A trust document is sometimes referred to as an indenture or trust indenture, which means, historically, a deed to which two or more persons are parties.

Trust property includes the assets that have been transferred to the trust by the trust maker. It is also called the trust principal, trust estate, or the Latin term trust corpus, which means trust body.

The trustee is the person or institution who is left in charge of carrying out the trust maker's instructions for the disposition of property contained in the trust. If there is more than one trustee, they are called co-trustees.

A testamentary trust is any type of trust that is created as part of your will and it does not take effect until after your death. You can cancel or change the trust, assuming you are competent, right up until your death.

A living trust is a trust that is created, funded, and can take effect while you are still alive.

The law states that no trust shall fail for lack of a trustee. If no trustee has been named in the trust document, the local courts having jurisdiction over trusts will name a trustee.

What is the purpose of a trust?

A trust allows you some control over what happens to your assets when you die and may result in tax savings.

When you leave property in a will that does not contain trust provisions, you leave it outright and there is no way to monitor, control or influence what your beneficiary does with the property. Trusts, of which there are many different kinds with different purposes, contain your instructions. They are under the control of the trustee that you named, and do allow you to exert some control from the grave, so to speak. With a trust, there is flexibility and a variety of arrangements possible. If, for instance, you were leaving a large sum of money to your son who was in his teens when you died, you could specify that his expenses are paid out of the interest, while the principal would be preserved until his marriage, or until he wished to buy a house, go to college or have children. Or you can establish a trust that takes care of expenses for your son and makes the entire inheritance available when he reaches a specific age, or, makes none of the principal available—passing it on to his children when he dies. In a trust, you can also simply leave the decision making to the trustee.

Trusts may serve another function as well—reducing estate taxes, leaving more for your beneficiaries. For instance, your property can be left in trust for your grandchildren, allowing their parents—your children—control over the property during their lifetime but not ownership. This technique will cause the generation-skipping transfer tax to apply and a competant accountant must allocate this unique credit.

With some trusts, you can direct income from your property, while you are alive, to someone in a lower tax bracket, thus saving yourself income taxes. See page 71 for more information on the kinds of trusts that offer tax-saving benefits.

Your property should be in a trust if...

- You want to maintain some control over the disposition of your property after you have died.
- Your beneficiaries are minors (the trust can end at adulthood or continue).
- Your beneficiaries are incompetent, irresponsible, or simply imprudent.
- You want to save estate taxes on the estates of future generations.
- You want to keep particular property in the family.

Leaving Property to a Minor

If you were to leave property to a minor in your will without establishing a trust, the courts will establish a trust for them and appoint a trustee who will have to make decisions without your instruction. In some states, the state has a custodian who holds the property of minors in associate accounts.

What are the limitations of a trust?

You can't see into the future.

While a trust allows you to reach into the future and control how, when and to whom your property is disbursed, it does not allow you to look into the future and know what successes or challenges your beneficiary will encounter. It is for this reason that estate planners generally recommend that, when planning the trust, you provide as much flexibility as possible in the instructions you leave, without undermining your desires. No matter how carefully an estate plan might be worked out today, it is impossible to look 20 or 30 years into the future and know what challenges will face your beneficiaries, or to know what circumstances will affect the usefulness of your gift. It is not uncommon for the long-term outcome of a trust to turn out to be quite different from what the trust maker originally intended.

In addition, a testamentary trust has one major limitation when compared to living trusts. Property which is the subject of a testamentary trust does not avoid probate, but must be approved for inclusion in the trust by the probate judge, with payment of the usual probate costs and fees. It is for this reason that more and more people are turning to living trusts.

Trusts, which are emerging as increasingly popular estate planning tools today, are at least 4,000 years old. The Babylonians historical Code of Hammurabi makes reference to trusts—a full 3500 years before the English passed laws just allowing citizens to pass down property at death.

The colonists first brought the trust to America. Patrick Henry has been given the first recorded credit for drafting a trust on this continent, which he wrote for the governor of Virginia, Robert Morris. Thomas Jefferson used a trust to protect his property from his bankrupt son-in-law.

Two Kinds of Trusts

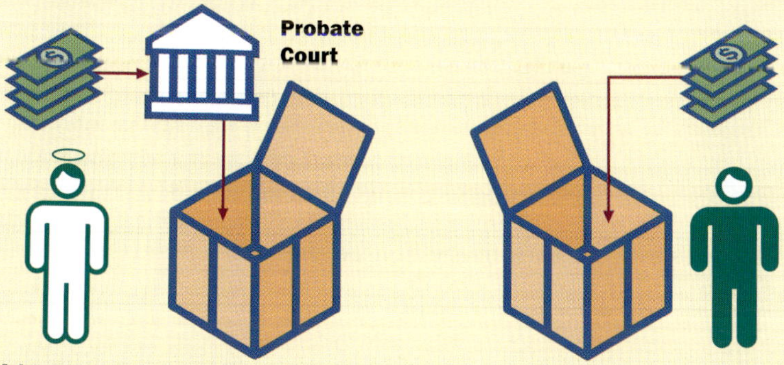

A testamentary trust is created as a part of your will and funded when you die. Probate court must approve what's included.

A living trust is created, funded, and administered while you are still alive. Probate court is avoided so costs are lower.

What is a living trust?

A living trust is a legal container in which assets are placed while the trust maker is still living.

Although **living trusts** are still relatively unknown to most people, they do not have to be difficult to understand or to use. A living trust is a trust created by an individual or couple into which assets are transferred. The living trust document will be in writing and, with its companion documents, can consist of a number of pages—from dozens to hundreds. Your trust can be named after you or you and your spouse (for example, the Mary (and John) Smith Trust—depending on whether you establish it yourself or together with your spouse. And, in fact, it can be named anything you want (the I Love My Kids Trust, for instance). With a living trust, you can be the trust maker, the trustee and the beneficiary—all three—to maintain control over your assets while you are alive. However, the living trust falls into the category of a **will substitute** because you can also pass on the trust property to beneficiaries upon your death.

What is the purpose of a living trust?

A living trust has many purposes and many features and functions. These include:

- Leaving your property to your beneficiaries, while still avoiding probate. Your beneficiaries will not have to wait for a court to approve the trust, as it is not required that it be filed with the court, nor will it be required that probate fees be paid on any property contained within. The terms of the trust will take effect immediately upon your death. If you have drafted your living trust with care, there should be no financial disruption for your family or unexpected consequences to your business. If you own property in more than one state, it allows your estate to avoid all the different court proceedings that would otherwise be necessary.

Your property should be in a living trust if...

- You want to save on probate fees when you die.
- You want privacy for your estate.
- You want to try out your estate plan before you die.
- You want your estate to be managed professionally.
- You own property in more than one state.

Living trusts are known by many names: revocable trusts, changeable trusts, inter vivos trusts, family trusts or grantor trusts (the name the IRS uses). These all refer to living trusts.

A will substitute is a document that is not a will, but that allows the maker to pass on property at their death.

- Ensuring privacy for your affairs. A living trust is a private document and not available for public view. Its terms will not be revealed to any but the beneficiaries and trustees named in the trust.
- Providing protection from contests. Since a living trust is not available for viewing, its terms are not readily discovered by unhappy relatives. Also, if a living trust is attacked, one of its best defenses is that it has been in existence for some time. The courts are therefore reluctant to interfere with something that has a history of performance.
- Providing protection of trust assets from beneficiaries' creditors. As long as your beneficiary's inheritance remains in a trust, creditors cannot access it.
- Insuring validity in every state, since it is a contract (unlike wills which are subject to varying laws and rules that govern them from state to state).
- Offering protection from public appraisal. While property left in a will requires public appraisal, the property in living trusts can be privately appraised by the trustees (who can be forbidden to reveal the value of trust assets to anyone except the trust beneficiaries).
- Having the ability to include all of your property, including real estate (even you own it as a joint tenant) and life insurance and other accounts or plans which have designated beneficiaries, unlike a will which cannot include these assets. (And since living trusts avoid probate—no probate fees would be due on any of these assets.) To take advantage of this possibility, you would put the real estate title of your joint tenancy property in the name of the trust as you would make the designated beneficiary your living trust.
- Allowing specific instructions for the care of your property, in the event of your mental or physical incapacity (see page 86). If you become disabled or incapacitated during your lifetime, the disability trustee that you established in your living trust will take over your affairs.

Effective Date for a Living Trust

Unlike the testamentary trust that takes effect upon your death, the living trust takes effect as soon as it is written and signed. You—the trust maker—have immediate control over the trust, unless you have named someone else as the trustee.

Get professional help in preparing your living trust documents. A living trust can be complex and lengthy. It is important that the terms and instructions be as clear, detailed and comprehensive as possible and meet all legal requirements. If you or your successor can't understand it, it will be difficult to carry out its terms.

There are two trusts that are sometimes confused with living trusts, but they are not the same:

- **The Constitutional Family Trust was a poor legal attempt at getting out of paying income taxes which is now forbidden by the IRS.**
- **The Clifford Trust is a special form of trust that shifts property income to one's children, for instance, who are in a lower tax bracket.**

Misconceptions about Living Trusts

Misconception: Some people fear that once assets are placed in a living trust, they will lose control over their assets, or that the surviving spouse will lose control over the assets that are passed on to him or her.

Truth: By naming yourself (and your spouse) as the trustee(s), you maintain full control over the property in a living trust and depending on the contents of the trust, some control over your property even once you have died. While alive, you can buy, sell, trade, invest, give away, earn income from, and manipulate your assets, just as you would without a trust. Similarly, you will still pay any taxes due on the property or its income and pay any related debts, just as you would without a trust.

Misconception: My estate is too small to warrant creating a living trust.

Truth: Studies have indicated that smaller estates are hit even harder by probate than larger estates, making a living trust even more essential.

Creating a living trust is not enough to gain its full benefit. An empty trust is useless. You must also **fund** it, that is, transfer your property into it, by **re-titling** the ownership of property. For a trust to be truly effective in avoiding probate and minimizing taxation, all of your assets must be placed into it. Re-titling normally requires that someone be notified of the change in the title.

What additional features does a living trust have?

- A living trust can be created by a single trust maker or two people as joint trust makers.
- A living trust is set up and takes effect during the trust makers' lives and the trust makers usually name themselves as trustees, thus maintaining control over their assets. To the extent that they use the assets in the trust, they are their own beneficiary.
- Upon death, the control of the trust goes into the hands of one or more successor trustees who were (carefully) selected by the trust maker(s).
- Successor trustees must follow instructions left in the living trust documents.
- The instructions concerning ownership, management and distribution of property, after death, cannot be changed or altered by the successor trustee, as long as they are not illegal.
- A living trust can be drafted to benefit any number of people, in any number of ways, allowing the trust maker to determine exactly how the estate will be managed and distributed even over a period of several lifetimes.

What are the limitations of a living trust?

There are estate planning specialists who have difficulty finding any disadvantages in a living trust, assuming that the trust is well written, properly funded (assets properly titled in the name of the trust), and accompanied by a well-designed estate planning program. Although in the long run living trusts can save your estate large sums of money by avoiding probate fees, initially they can be more costly to prepare than wills.

The initial cost of preparing a living trust can be two or three times the cost of preparing an ordinary will. The expense of probate and other potentially unnecessary taxes and fees after your death would probably exceed the cost of preparing a living trust.

Although living trusts avoid probate, there is still cost involved in settling an estate. Settling the average or small estate with a living trust can sometimes be done by the surviving spouse or other beneficiaries—although some advice about trust administration is recommended, especially if a state tax return is required.

Will a living trust protect my assets from creditors? Despite some claims, a living trust will not shield you from creditors. Property titled in the name of your living trust will be treated the same as any other property by your creditors during your lifetime. If, however, you are a beneficiary of a trust set up by someone else, the funds in the trust cannot be seized by your creditors unless you withdraw the funds.

Will a living trust protect me from income taxes? When you re-title and place assets into your living trust, it creates no change in your personal income tax status. The IRS will treat the property as though you still own it as an individual. During your lifetime, a living trust offers no income tax advantage.

Congress changes estate tax laws approximately every 5 years. The person or firm who prepares your living trust should notify you if any changes would benefit you and require alterations in your trust. Also, your trust should be originally organized so as to make review and changes relatively easy to make.

Living trusts do not offer any income tax advantage during your lifetime. Sometimes living trusts are confused with irrevocable trusts (see page 79), which do offer protection from both personal income and estate taxes.

The Pros and Cons

Estate Planning Benefit	No Estate Plan	Will Only	Living Trust
Avoids delays of probate court	No	No	**Yes**
Avoids probate fees for attorneys, executor, appraiser	No	No	**Yes**
Gives you an opportunity to minimize taxes	No	**Yes**	**Yes**
Provides for incapacity or disability	No	No	**Yes**
Avoids public disclosure of financial affairs	No	No	**Yes**
Operates without court supervision	No	No	**Yes**
Avoids interruption of family business	No	**Yes**	**Yes**
Offers control over your estate for generations	No	No*	**Yes**
Allows for charitable giving	No	**Yes**	**Yes**
All signed copies are valid	N.A.	No	**Yes**
Avoids conservatorship proceedings	No	No	Sometimes
Is valid in any state	No	**Yes**	**Yes**

** Unless a testamentary trust is established as part of the will.*

Storing Your Trust Documents

Store your living trust with your other important papers. Consider a safety deposit box or fireproof box. It is most important that the successor trustee you appoint knows where the trust document is and has access to it. You may want to give copies to your successor trustee or beneficiaries. You should never sign or notarize any copies unless they are done on the same date as the original.

Q

When I change the ownership of my property to a trust, will it be reappraised for property taxes?

A

No. As long as it is just the form of title that changes and not the names of the owners, funding your living trust is a non-tax event.

Q

When transferring titles, will I have to show my living trust documents to prove it exists?

A

Sometimes. However, your attorney can prepare an Affidavit of Trust. The affidavit is adequate in almost every case to change a title.

How do I revise and update my living trust? Like a will, a living trust is easy to update and change. Although, informal changes on the original trust itself are not recommended as they may be hard to defend should someone challenge them. Changes, or amendments, are performed with a dated written document called an **Amendment to the (Name of Trust).** The amendment should repeat any clauses being deleted. They should also state what is being added to the trust. Like the trusts themselves, they require a date and a signature which has been witnessed and notarized. Since amendments can be accidentally misplaced and the fact that they exist not readily known, they should only be used for very minor changes.

When more than minor amendments are needed, a new trust document known as a **Restatement of Trust** is prepared. This is a new document that incorporates the changes, but it keeps the trust name so that assets do not require a name change on their titles. The old documents can be destroyed to avoid confusion. The name on these trusts would be something like the Restatement of Mary Smith Trust dated October 10, 1972. This date is the date of the original trust. The restatement would then be signed and dated with the current date of signing.

When and how does a living trust come to an end? A living trust comes to an end when you revoke it or when it has distributed all its assets. Also, the laws governing the operation of a trust—including the length of time property can be held in trust—vary from state to state. While a trust can reach into the future, touching future generations, there is no state that will allow a trust to operate indefinitely, except in the case of charitable or employee trusts. In most states, a trust can be created to last for about 121 years, at which point all remaining assets in the trust must be distributed. No formal termination document is required to end a living trust if the trust property has all been distributed.

How do I revoke my trust? Revocation must be done in a written document, signed by the trust maker. A shared trust can usually be revoked by either trust maker any time. In the case of divorce, one co-maker can revoke his or her interest and withdraw his or her property from the trust, as determined in the divorce proceedings. If a trust maker wishes to revoke a trust to create a new one in its place, the new trust should have a different name to avoid any possible confusion. For instance, something as simple as adding the Roman numeral II to the name. When a trust is revoked, it is very important to transfer all property titles into the new trust, or back into your own name if there is no new trust. It is also prudent to track down all copies of the old trust and destroy them. Given the work involved in creating the trust, revoking a trust should be a last resort. Many changes can be handled by amendments and restatements.

You usually have some choice as to the state in which you create your living trust. The only rule is that the trust have some connection with the designated state: for instance, the location of real estate held in the trust, or the residence of either the trust maker or the trustee.

States That Require Registration of a Living Trust

Colorado
Registration is required when trust maker dies if distribution of property is delayed.

Tennessee
Registration applies only to the removal or resignation of a trustee.

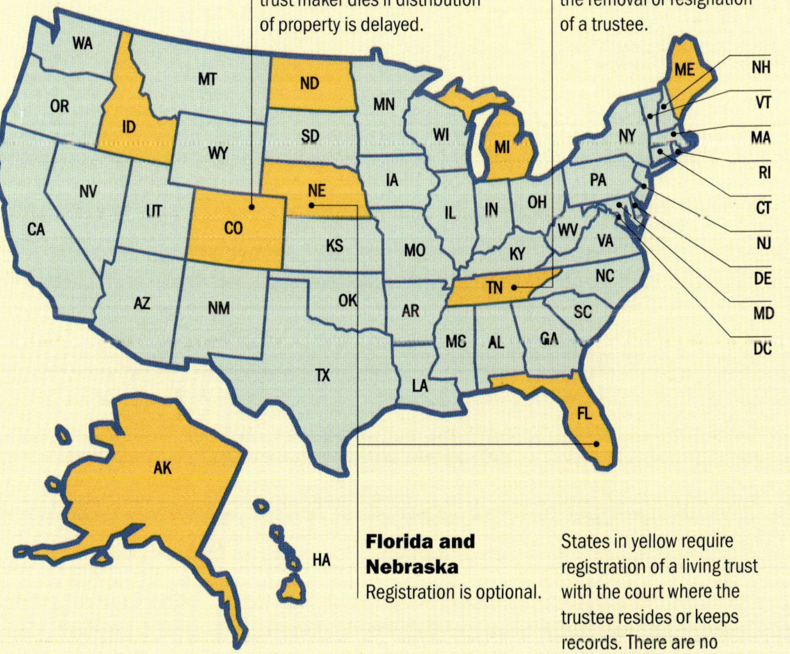

Florida and Nebraska
Registration is optional.

States in yellow require registration of a living trust with the court where the trustee resides or keeps records. There are no penalties or legal consequences if you don't.

How are living trusts structured to meet my estate planning needs?

Living trusts can be structured in an infinite number of ways, using various sub-trusts. Together with the additional documents that most estate planners would recommend, a living trust can meet most of your estate planning needs.

There is no limit to the number of sub-trusts that can be created within a single living trust. Each of the sub-trusts can have different terms and conditions for the distribution of property placed into them and the timing of the distribution. The property in each of the sub-trusts can flow down into other sub-trusts at specific times or events, as instructed by the trust maker.

Some common trust structures are referred to by attorneys as the A Trust, the A-B Trust, the A-B-C Trust and the partner A-A Trust. Each serves a different purpose, depending on your personal situation.

Chapter 7

What is an A Trust?

An A Trust is for you if you are not married or you and your spouse have a small estate.

With an **A Trust**, when you die, all of the assets in your will or living trust go into one trust in the name of the surviving spouse or other beneficiaries (in which case the trust becomes irrevocable—unchangeable). This trust **can** be used by married couples, but **must** be used in the event you are single, divorced or widowed.

In estates valued at less than the **estate tax exemption** amount, the entire estate will go to a single trust for the benefit of beneficiaries, since there will be neither probate fees nor estate taxes to pay. On any amounts over the estate tax exemption, estate taxes would be payable. The A Trust works also for married couples whose estate is valued at much less than estate tax exemption amount. In these cases, the A Trust is usually left to the surviving spouse, although that is not required.

Estate Tax Exemptions

Estate taxes are payable on any amounts over the exemption amount. The applicable exemption amounts will be changing through the year 2006 as noted below.

Year	Exemption Amount
2000-2001	$ 675,000
2002-2003	$ 700,000
2004	$ 850,000
2005	$ 950,000
2006	$ 1,000,000

A Trust

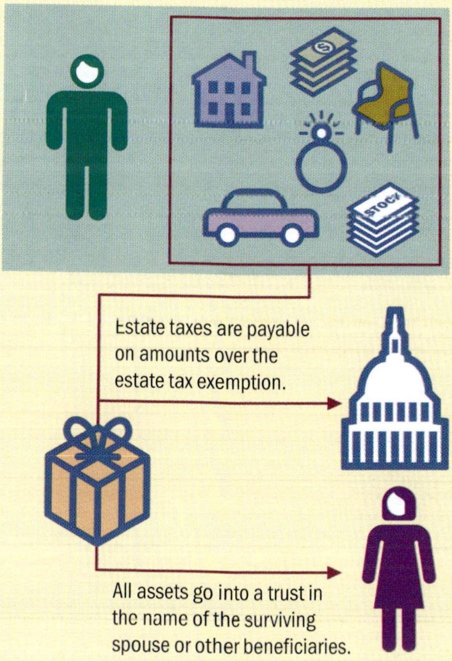

For married couples, many estate planners recommend the A-B Trust (see page 73), no matter what the size of their estate.

What is an A-A trust?

A-A Trusts are not legal in all states.

An A–A Trust can be used if you want to share a living trust with someone who is not your spouse.

This trust is primarily two single A trusts blended together. Both parties may own property separately, which is identified as such, and they may own property together. Although both parties may have common interests and assets, they usually have different objectives when it comes to the disbursement of their property when they die. They often do not have heirs in common and want to leave their estate to entirely different families.

A-A Trust

A-A trusts allow individuals to maintain property separately and to control how their property is disbursed—usually to two different sets of heirs.

An A–B Trust is used to share a living trust with your spouse.

A-B Trusts are used when a married couple is involved in the will or living trust. Two sub-trusts are actually created—**Trust A** which goes to the last spouse to die (the surviving spouse) and **Trust B** which becomes a part of the estate of the first spouse to die (the decedent).

How does an A-B Trust work? Upon the death of the first spouse, a portion of the couple's assets will flow down into Trust B (the decedent's trust). The rest of the couple's assets goes to the survivor's trust—Trust A. Usually, Trust B contains the amount of the estate tax exemption, with the remainder going to Trust A. Depending on the preferences of the couple, the Trust A usually has liberal terms and conditions. In fact the A portion does not have to go into a trust but can go directly to the surviving spouse.

The surviving partner can retain full control over, not just Trust A, but also Trust B while he or she is still alive. He or she can receive income from the assets in Trust B and may be able to tap the principal if permitted by the terms of the trust. But A-B Trusts can also have all kinds of limits, restrictions, and conditions, if the couple so chooses.

When the surviving partner dies, Trust B passes to the beneficiaries as designated in the will or living trust document (although they could have been receiving distribution from the trust even during the lifetime of the survivor, depending on the terms of the trust). The assets remaining in Trust A will either be distributed according to the terms of the Trust A or, if permitted, the terms of the surviving spouse's will or living trust. Each of the trusts can leave up to the maximum estate tax exemption amount before any federal estate taxes are due, and if any estate taxes are due, they are not payable until both partners have died.

What is an A-B Trust?

A-B Trusts are also known as marital trusts or bypass trusts. A-B Trusts allow amounts above the estate tax exemption to be sheltered.

PUT NOT YOUR TRUST IN MONEY, BUT PUT YOUR MONEY IN TRUST.

—OLIVER WENDELL HOLMES

There are no citizenship requirements for the makers of an A-B Trust. However, use of the unlimited marital deduction will be limited (see discussion on QDOTs on page 77).

Are A-B Trusts revocable? Both Trust A and B are revocable—or changeable—while the trustmaker is still alive. However, upon the death these trusts become irrevocable—unchangeable.

What are the benefits of an A-B Trust?

- It better protects the first decedent's desires for the final distribution of his or her share of the couple's property because the first decedent's trust becomes irrevocable upon his or her death. If, for instance, the remaining partner were to remarry, after his or her death the property in Trust B would be protected and still go on to the beneficiaries named in Trust B. While the surviving partner may maintain some control over Trust B, he or she can be prevented from changing the beneficiaries or other terms of the trust. This is particularly useful when the first partner to die has children who would not normally receive anything from the surviving spouse–as in the case of children from a previous marriage.

A-B Trust

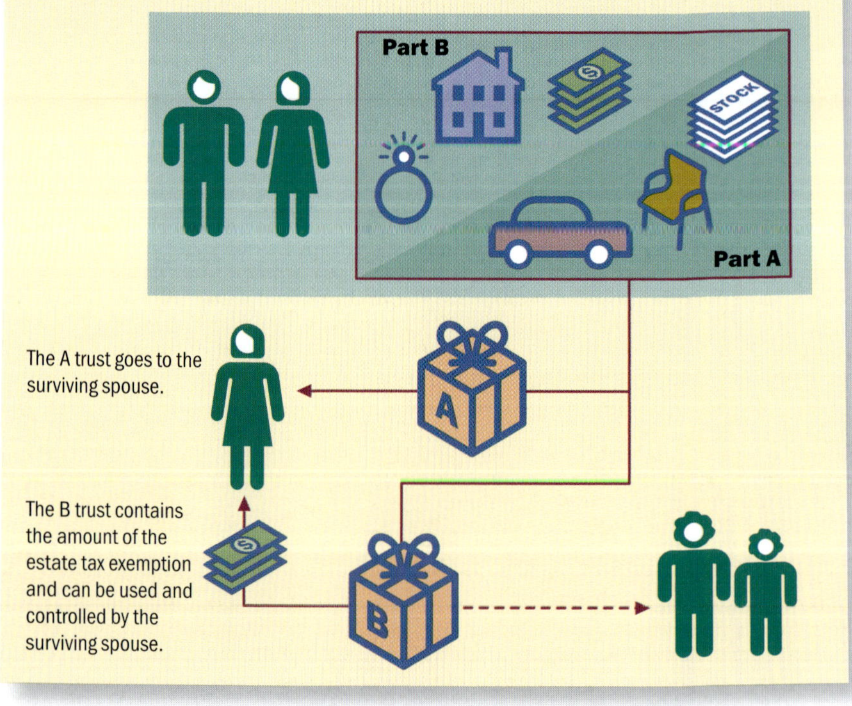

- It takes better advantage of the federal estate tax exemption to which each marriage partner is entitled. While most married couples should consider this type of trust, it is particularly important to those with estates which have the potential to grow over the estate tax exemption amount, as these trusts can be used to reduce or eliminate federal estate taxes.

Normally, one spouse can leave an unlimited amount to the surviving spouse, without paying estate taxes. This is called an **unlimited marital deduction.** However when the second spouse dies, any part of his or her estate (now made up of both spouse's estates) over the estate tax exemption is subject to federal taxation and the estate tax exemption that the first spouse was entitled to is wasted. A-B trusts avoid this problem. Upon the death of the first partner, a couple can leave up to the estate tax exemption amount of their property, federal estate tax free, in Trust B for the family or other beneficiaries who will receive it after the death of the second partner. It can allow the surviving partner use of the property, but also allows the couple to utilize the estate tax exemption of the first to die.

An A-B trust could be useful even in smaller estates because, although an estate might today be worth much less than the estate tax exemption, over the years it can appreciate substantially. As an estate grows in value, an A-B trust ensures that, as long as the estate of the remaining partner doesn't grow to be over the estate tax exemption amount, no estate tax will be due for either of them.

For this reason, couples place in the B Trust—for the first to die—those assets most likely to appreciate: for instance, their real estate. This would serve to insulate the growth on those assets from future possible estate taxation—as long as they were valued at under the estate tax exemption at the time of death of the first partner. Whatever is in Trust B can continue to grow in value, but when it is passed on to beneficiaries, the value used for estate taxation purposes, is the value at the time of death of the first spouse, which could have been many years earlier, before inflation and before appreciation has increased the property's value.

Estate Value

An estate can be expected to double in value in a period of 10 years, just from inflation alone.

Unlimited marital deduction is available to all married couples who are American citizens. It allows one spouse to leave the entire contents of his or her estate to the surviving spouse estate tax free, no matter what the size of the estate.

Fiduciary responsibility requires trustees to handle the property in the trust responsibly and in keeping with the wishes of the trust maker and the laws governing the trust. Examples of fiduciary abuse include gambling the money away or transferring the assets out of the trust.

Will the surviving partner lose the benefit and control of the assets left in an A-B Trust?
Not necessarily. One of the concerns that couples have about this type of trust is that it could potentially cause hardship. Understanding the flexibility of these trusts is helpful. Both spouses together establish the terms of the trust and can make it as strict or as liberal as they like. In a more liberal trust, the beneficiaries can be made contingent beneficiaries; that is, they receive only whatever assets are left in the trust, if any, upon the death of the surviving spouse.

Note, however, that contingent beneficiaries do have rights and the surviving spouse, as trustee, would have a **fiduciary responsibility** to protect those rights. Ultimately, the amount of control the surviving spouse will have depends on what terms and conditions both spouses set for the trust when they create it.

Rights of the Surviving Spouse Over an A-B Trust

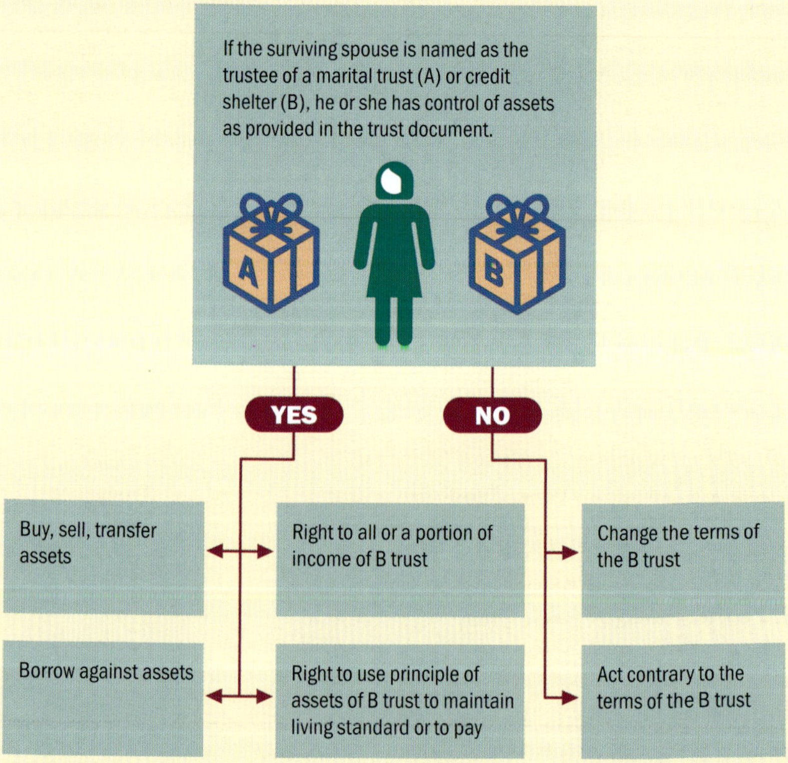

A QTIP Trust is for couples with a taxable estate and children from previous marriages.

A **Qualified Terminable Interest Property (QTIP) Trust** is used to direct the distribution of the entire estate of the first spouse to die. The QTIP Trust is not appropriate if you wish assets to go to beneficiaries, other than your partner, immediately after your death.

How does a QTIP trust work? Upon the death of the first partner, the amount of the estate tax exemption goes into Trust B. The remaining amount of the decedent's share of the couple's estate flows into a QTIP Trust. The surviving spouse receives the income (and sometimes principal) from the property held in the QTIP Trust, and when he or she dies, the assets go to the beneficiaries specified in the trust document.

This is commonly used when couples have children who would not necessarily be beneficiaries of the surviving spouse. The beneficiaries do not receive the property in the QTIP Trust until the death of the second partner, and any estate taxes would not be due until then. Taxes would be based on the value of the property at the time of the first decedent's death, thus protecting beneficiaries from paying taxes on the gain.

What is a QTIP trust?

Qualified Domestic Trusts (QDOT)

If you or your spouse is not a U.S. citizen, a QDOT should be used. The unlimited marital deduction is not allowed when the surviving spouse is not a U.S. citizen, except when property passing to the surviving spouse is in a QDOT. Technically, in a QDOT, the assets do not pass to the non-citizen spouse but remain in trust for their use.

These trusts are a variation of the QTIP trust and require that the person named as the trustee or a co-trustee be an American citizen, in order for the trust to qualify as a vehicle for deferring estate taxes. The American trustee's primary responsibility is to pay the appropriate tax upon the death of the surviving spouse, no matter where the surviving spouse is located at the time of death.

QTIP Trust

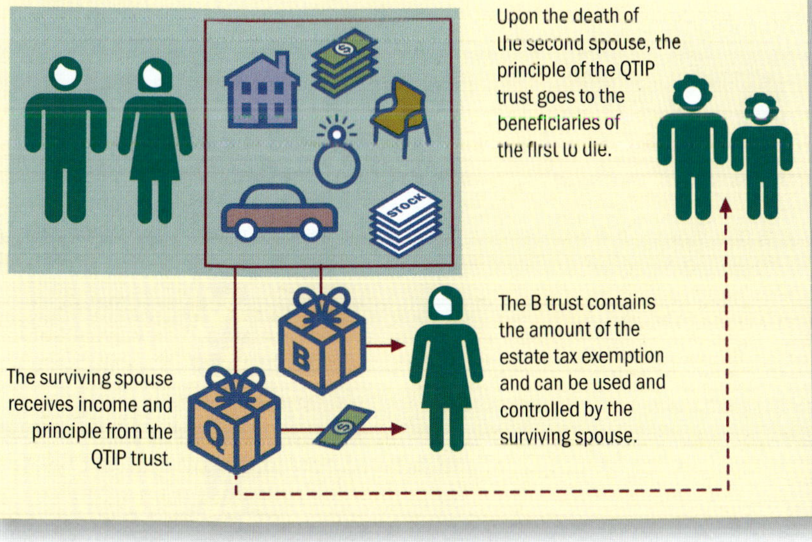

What are common and separate trusts?

Gifts to Minors

The Uniform Gift to Minor's Act requires that the trustee hand over inherited property to the child when she or he reaches age 18 to 21 (depending on the state). For larger gifts, a common trust or separate trust is preferable to simply giving a gift or bequest to a minor upon your death.

Balancing Inheritance With Need

If each child had a separate trust of the same value, one child could run out of money much more quickly (due to special needs) than the others and would not be able to access the funds in the siblings' trusts.

A common trust will provide for your children who will need care, as a group.

A common trust comes into existence for your children after the death of both spouses. Since it does not split up your estate before the future needs of your children are known, it allows trustees to access the entire estate to address the individual needs of each of your children. This trust terminates at a time (or when certain conditions occur) which you specify in the trust. Some children, due to their age or situation, will require more of your property than others. For instance, an 18 year-old will probably need less support than a 7 year old. If the estate is large enough, common trusts can instruct a trustee to release funds for specified purposes to adult children, while waiting for the younger children to reach maturity. At the end of this trust, you can instruct that any remaining property be split in some fashion into separate trusts or distributed outright to the children.

Separate trusts take care of a specific beneficiary.

Separate trusts would be most appropriate if all of your children are adults or the common trust comes to an end, but you don't want outright distribution of your estate. Separate trusts allow you to exert some control over how the property in the trust is managed. They can be created immediately upon the first death, or can wait until the death of the surviving spouse.

Separate trusts should include instructions on how the trustee should administer them and distribute funds. Your instructions can state whatever you wish—that you want your children liberally provided for, or that only health, education, support, and maintenance of the children be provided. The trust should also state the method of distribution and when funds should be disbursed.

Trusts provide your children with the funds when needed, but also protect those funds they don't yet need from creditors.

What else can I accomplish with a trust?

While you cannot always eliminate taxes, you can accomplish just about anything else that is within the law.

The trusts mentioned previously are some of the more commonly used trusts, but there are many more—too many to include here. There are trusts that can save you up to hundreds of thousands of dollars in estate taxes, depending on the size of your estate, and that can even save you income taxes while reducing the size of your taxable estate. You can control what property goes to whom, at what time, and in what manner. You can use a generation-skipping trust to leave up to $1,030,000 to your grandchildren, thus avoiding some of the double taxation that would occur had your children—their parents—inherited it first, paid estate taxes on it, and then passed it on to their children, again subjecting the property to estate taxes.

Whatever it is you want to do, there is a trust vehicle that can help you do it. You can support a charity by donating your home, thus reducing your taxable estate, but still live in it for the rest of your life with a **Charitable Gift Annuity.** With a Charitable Remainder Trust you can make a gift of an asset to a charity, also reducing your taxable estate, yet continue to receive an income from that asset up until your death. Or you can remove the proceeds of your life insurance from your taxable estate, and designate what the proceeds should be used for with an **Irrevocable Life Insurance Trust.** Proceeds could be assigned to pay estate taxes and other costs before distribution to your beneficiaries. The first step is to decide what you want to accomplish and then, with the help of your advisors, you can choose the tools that would best carry out your wishes.

Irrevocable trusts are often used to save income tax and estate taxes. To gain the tax benefits of these trusts, you cannot be the trust maker and the beneficiary too. Unlike living trusts, irrevocable trusts cannot be altered once they are made. But such a trust can support a family member or a charity and can provide an income for you if you so choose.

WE MAKE A LIVING BY WHAT WE GET, BUT WE MAKE A LIFE BY WHAT WE GIVE.

—SIR WINSTON CHURCHILL

What other documents do I need in my estate plan?

There are a number of legal documents which are considered to be separate from a will or living trust. They are not legally required, but with the right documents you can avoid complications, delays, and extra expenses, and ensure that there are more assets for your beneficiaries.

Chapter 8

How do I keep my property separate in joint estate planning?

Separate Property Agreement

A Separate Property Agreement spells out what property is yours and what belongs to your spouse.

A Separate Property Agreement lists the property which is legally separate property, by virtue of one partner receiving a gift or inheritance, or ownership of property from before the marriage.

If my spouse and I have separate property, how can we include it in the estate plan without making it joint property? Depending on the laws of your state, you may be able to create a list of separate assets and include it as part of your estate plan. A trust is just a contract between two people and therefore, any assets both parties agree are separate are recognized as such. Even though the property will be titled or formally named in the name of the trust—the John and Betty Smith Trust, for instance—the assets included in this document will retain their separate character. The property is being brought together for both parties benefit, and at the death of one spouse, his or her separate property can be put in the B Trust or into the QTIP Trust (see pages 73–77). Upon the second spouse's death, however, that separate property will go to the beneficiaries, as listed in the trust by the spouse whose separate property it was. Upon his or her death, it is also possible for each spouse to simply leave their separate assets to other beneficiaries, removing them from the trust completely or in part. Divorce courts generally recognize Separate Property Agreements which are correctly executed, provided that neither spouse has done anything, intentionally or accidentally, to change the legal character of the separate asset.

Blended Families and Inheritance

Spouses who have children from previous marriages often find the Separate Property Agreement useful.

Separate Property Agreement

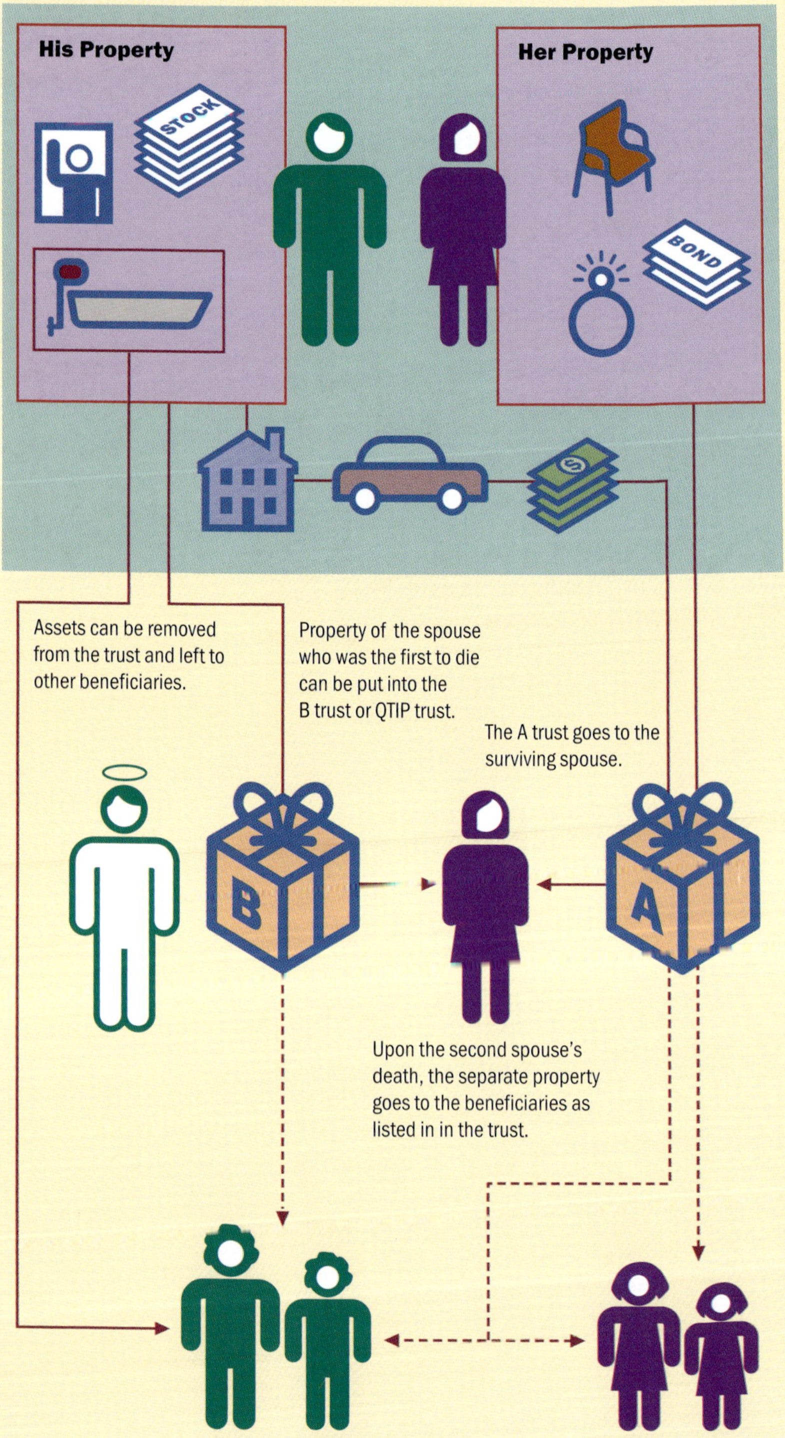

Business Succession Plan

A well-crafted business succession plan can help to ensure your business is carried on as you would like.

If you have a family business, your estate plan will not work the way you intended it to unless you also plan for the business. Many business owners do not give a lot of thought to what will happen to their business should they die suddenly. Will your family take over? Are they willing and able to? Will your associates buy your interest? Will a competitor take advantage of your company's weakened state and buy your family out for pennies on the dollar? Will the company go bankrupt? It can be just as important to have a business succession plan as it is to have a business startup plan. The best personal estate plan can be ruined if your survivors are forced to prop up, re-organize, or sell your business unexpectedly. And if you have only a will or no estate plan at all, your business will be tied up in probate, during which time it may go bankrupt anyway because then it cannot be sold, liquidated or transferred without court approval.

A business succession plan allows you to decide who, if anyone, is going to run your business and who is going to benefit from the value of your business. It can also be flexible, allowing periodic review and adjustments in response to changes in your business as it grows and evolves. Although it is good to have some agreements as to what happens in the event of your death, it does not mean that you can ignore your business succession plan when forming your estate plan. If it is ignored, your business will surely end up in probate court resulting in expenses and delays and potentially interfering with other elements of your estate plan.

What if I have a family business?

Your ability to control your business interest will be determined or limited by the form of your business. Is it a sole proprietorship, a partnership, a small corporation, or a large one? Are there shareholders? Is there a buy/sell agreement that takes effect at your death or when you are disabled? Businesses formed on a handshake are not reliable as estate planning tools.

A Life Insurance Trust can be used to provide non-taxable funds to help stabilize your business after your death (see page 79). If you anticipate that your business will not survive past your death, there are planning options for you that will not leave your survivors in the lurch, dealing with estate taxes and probate.

What if I have a living trust and some assets get left out?

Pour-Over Will

A pour-over will adds property to a living trust that was accidentally left out.

Although the living trust is, in effect, a will substitute which spells out to whom, when, and how your assets are to be distributed, you still should have an accompanying document commonly referred to as a pour-over will (simply titled Will). A pour-over will is made up of the following elements:

1. It identifies you, the will maker, by name, your spouse, and all children and step-children (if you desire).

2. It revokes any prior wills and their codicils.

3. It pours into the living trust any major assets, or personal and household property, that had been left out of it. Personal and house-hold effects should primarily be transferred into a living trust by way of a document called an Assignment of Furniture, Furnishings, and Personal Effects (see page 86).

4 It establishes an executor who will be responsible for taking those properties left out of the trust through probate. Once the probate process is finished, the executor can transfer whatever assets are remaining into the living trust to be disposed of according to the instructions in the trust.

5 A pour-over will can also name the guardians of any dependents and their property, although a better way to do this is through a document called Appointment of Guardian (see page 87).

Probate is not avoided for assets that must be transferred to your trust through a pour-over will. Keep the pour-over will as a backup but don't procrastinate putting your assets into your living trust before you die! The pour-over will is a useful catch-all and should be part of all living trusts, but it should be relied upon only when unavoidable.

If you die with a very large estate, the potential for suits against you is greatly increased. Some estate planners recommend leaving a certain amount of money out of your trust, thus putting it through probate, because once the probate process is finished the window of opportunity to sue the estate closes.

If you wish to disinherit a child, in most states that fact must be stated in both the living trust and the pour-over will.

Bing Crosby had a living trust for his very large estate, but $1 million was probated specifically to ensure that any suits against his estate were covered and could not drag on indefinitely.

What about my personal property?

Assignment of Furniture, Furnishings, and Personal Effects transfers tangible personal property without a detailed inventory.

Personal Property Memorandum allows you to leave specific items to specific people, if you so wish.

Gifts to Heirs... Before They're Born

My grandmother, Thora Quam, was an inspirational person who took great care and loved each one of her seven grandchildren greatly. Long before we were born, she decided how she would pass down to us her most precious things–such as her engagement and wedding rings, and her wedding dress. She wrote down a list indicating that, for instance, the second granddaughter would receive the engagement ring and the first grandson would receive my grandfather's ring. The fact that she was thinking about us even before we were born made us feel special and it completely removed any disagreement over who was to receive what of our grandmother's keepsakes. I wear her engagement ring every day.

—Lois Quam, CEO, Ovations, Minneapolis, MN.

Assignment of Personal Property

You can specify how your personal property is handled.

How do I ensure my personal property is included in my trust? An **Assignment of Furniture, Furnishings, and Personal Effects** document is used for personal belongings that usually do not have ownership papers such as a title. Given the cost of things these days, it is quite easy for people to accumulate many personal effects that total quite a large sum—more than the maximum amount allowed before probate becomes necessary. This amount varies from state to state. Personal effects include furniture, jewelry, silverware and china, books, and collections of various sorts. With this document, you may transfer all existing and all future personal property into the living trust.

How do I make sure the right people receive my personal property? A **Personal Property Memorandum** becomes an attachment to the will or living trust and allows you to make specific gifts of personal property to whomever you choose. For example, you might want to leave a specific piece of jewelry, photos, mementos, books, letters, musical instruments, artwork, or clothing to particular individuals who may not otherwise be named as beneficiaries. This memorandum allows you to express your generosity in a very personal way which will have special meaning to those who receive the gift.

The personal property memorandum should number and describe each item and clearly indicate the name and address of the recipient. Then each page should be numbered, dated, and signed. A personal property memorandum can be changed at any time before your death. It does not need to be witnessed, notarized, or reviewed by an attorney.

Care of Dependents

You can name a guardian to care for your children in the event of your death and offer instructions for their care.

How do I appoint guardians for my minor children or dependents? As mentioned earlier, a will is one vehicle for appointing guardians for dependents. Some estate planners prefer the **Appointment of Guardian,** a short document to serve this purpose. This document can be used both for minor children and for adult children who are mentally or physically disabled. Since guardians may be responsible for your dependents until they reach the age of 21, depending on their age at your death, many years could elapse between your death and their maturity. For this reason, it is very important that you name alternate guardians, just in case something happens to the primary guardian you appoint or the guardian declines the appointment.

How do I offer instruction and guidance to my dependent's guardians? While there is no formal name for this type of document, it could be titled something like **A Letter to Our Children's Guardians.** Most people would have a great deal to say to those who may one day become the guardians of their children. These thoughts can take the form of firm suggestions or thoughts and observations about the children, their education, religion, activities, lifestyle or their upbringing in general. If you give them a copy now, it may also give you an opportunity to discuss the contents which will help insure that they understand them fully. However, some people prefer to wait and have the letter read only if the guardianship becomes a reality.

What about the care of my dependents?

The person you name as guardian does not necessarily need to be the trustee of your living trust.

To lose one parent... may be regarded as a misfortune; to lose both looks like carelessness.

—Oscar Wilde

What if I become incapacitated or incompetent?

If you were to give General Power of Attorney (GPOA) to someone (usually a spouse or an adult child but it could be anyone), it gives the holder the right to completely run your financial affairs. Legally, GPOAs are supposed to end if you were to become incompetent, but it is difficult to prevent the holder from continuing to use it and usually the holder does continue. Many attorneys consider this to be very dangerous. GPOAs are often at the root of theft and mismanagement.

Court-Appointed Conservator

If you become incapacitated and have not legally appointed someone to make personal care, medical or financial decisions for you, the court will appoint a conservator–usually a member of your family, or sometimes a public official. While the process varies from state to state, it usually begins by someone else filing a petition with the court asking for appointment. A conservator appointed to handle your personal affairs is called the "conservator of the person," while the one appointed to handle your financial affairs is named "conservator of the estate." Conservatorships can be expensive, can take many months to complete and do require work. You lose all control of your personal and financial affairs and it is possible that your loved ones may not be the ones awarded this role. You also lose privacy since these proceedings are public and open for anyone to review.

Power of Attorney

You can give power of attorney to someone you trust and appoint a conservator.

What if I have a living trust and cannot transfer my assets due to incapacitation? A **Durable Special Power of Attorney for Funding** document allows you to empower someone you trust to place your property into your living trust should you be unable to do so, but does not give that person any other power or authority over your affairs. While an ordinary power of attorney you have granted someone automatically ends if you were to become incompetent, the durable power of attorney continues in such a case.

How can I ensure that I am personally cared for should I become unable to care for myself? With an **Appointment of Conservator** document, you can identify the person who will be responsible for ensuring your general safety and well being, should you be unable to do so yourself. For this role, you must choose a person you trust to make decisions which are in keeping with what you would want—the choice of caregivers, nursing homes, etc.—to provide you with the best and most humane care possible. The appointment of a conservator should not to be confused with the Durable Power of Attorney for Health Care, which addresses medical treatment decisions (see above), or the Competency Clause (see below), which addresses the care of your financial affairs.

How do I give another person authority to take care of my financial affairs, should I become incompetent? A Competency Clause can be added to your living trust so that if you were to lose competency due to illness (mental or physical), senility, or an accident, management of your financial affairs could continue. The person you name in the clause would be able to buy, sell or transfer your assets for you, pay bills and even collect any income on your behalf. You can specify that the physician attending you, plus another physician of your choice, can simply write a letter establishing your incompetence. Since it is part of a living trust, this clause is applicable in every state. While some people are concerned that abuse might occur, if they include a competency clause, this clause can actually protect them and their assets from unscrupulous people who exploit the elderly or the infirm. Should you become incompetent and not have this clause, your personal affairs, and very likely the personal affairs of your spouse can grind to a halt for months.

If you have no estate plan or only a will, and you become incapacitated, someone would have to petition the probate court to appoint a conservator to take care of you and your affairs. However, in a Living Trust, without a separate document, you can also simply appoint a disability trustee, making sure to include a definition of what constitutes disability, and a statement that when the disability ends, the trustee steps down. You should also include instructions for your care and the care of your affairs. This can make both the Appointment of Conservator and the Competency Clause unnecessary.

If you had been declared legally incompetent and regain your competency, the same doctors can certify your competency again by simply writing a letter to reinstate you. If you disagree with their decision, you have the right to have the courts determine your competency.

Someone to Watch Over Me

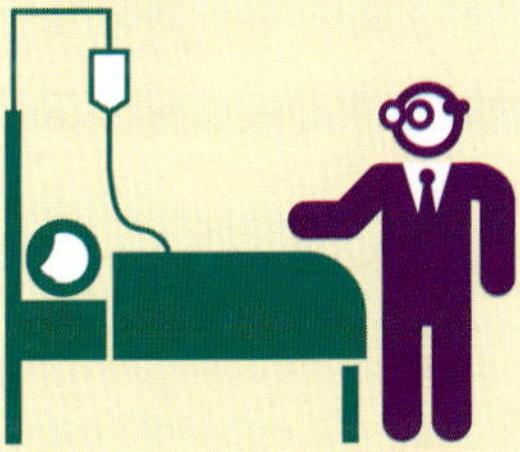

If you're out of action, someone you trust can direct your affairs. But you've got to plan ahead for this eventuality.

The Groucho Marx Story

Groucho Marx did not have a living trust nor a durable power of attorney for health care. His case was one of the most famous examples of the nightmare this problem can create. Groucho became weak and very forgetful in later years. Because he appeared to be unable to manage his affairs, he was considered legally incompetent and the courts had to appoint a conservator. The court process was lengthy with battles going on between his children, his girlfriend, and his banks. After dragging on, the battles were finally ended just before his death, at which point a battle in probate over his will ensued. A large portion of his estate was used up in both legal and probate fees.

Perhaps the worst was that while he was too weak to participate in the proceedings, he was thought to have been perfectly aware of what was going on around him. Throughout the trial, Groucho looked gloomy and at times he cried. Many believe that the stress of being wheeled into court day after day, hearing the most personal details of his life raked over, while the press and world turned the public proceedings into a circus, just hastened his death.

Can I prepare in advance for terminal illness?

In some states, a person may not make a living will within 5 days of being notified that they are terminally ill. However, when done without the pressure of illness or accident, the living will is usually a legally accepted document.

In some states, you can donate organs by filling out a form on the back of your driver's license. Some medical professionals have warned against this practice, however. They have observed that when your desire is known by attending doctors, by way of your license, and you are in a gray area between life and death, there is a temptation to take your vital organs prematurely to save someone else's life.

In some states, the DPAHC can include your thoughts and directives about life-sustaining measures, anatomical gifts, memorial arrangements, and even autopsy. This single document replaces several documents, and its scope and authority is determined by state law.

Advance Directive

You can document your wishes about the medical care you receive.

How do I give instructions ahead of time for my care if I should become terminally ill and unable to communicate? An **Advance Directive** is a legal document in which you state how you want to be treated if you become very ill and there is no reasonable hope for your recovery. Although laws vary from state to state, there are basically two kinds of advance directives: the **Durable Power of Attorney for Health Care** (DPAHC) or **Health Care Proxy** and a **Living Will.** You can have both.

The DPAHC grants other(s) the right to make medical decisions for you, should you be unable to do so yourself. If you so choose, you can limit or specify what decisions that person can make. The person granted this right is called the attorney in fact and should you choose to appoint more than one (you can appoint as many as you like), they are called co-attorneys in fact or co-agents.

The DPAHC is especially important for unmarried people since they do not have a spouse who can legally make decisions for them. In most states, but not all, adult children or parents can authorize treatment for each other if there is no spouse. In the case of married couples, the spouse is legally permitted to make medical decisions, but if both spouses were to become incapacitated at the same time, the problem would be the same for them as for an unmarried person. Many estate planners provide this document for all of their clients. Those who are married can designate their spouse as the attorney in fact with one or more people named as successor attorneys.

How do I give instructions regarding my right to die in case I become reliant on life-support systems? Today, with modern technology making great strides forward in lengthening and sustaining life, a Living Will is probably more important than ever. These documents contain what are popularly known as **right-to-die clauses** that state if your life is being sustained only by artificial means, it is your desire—a desire expressed when you were fully competent—that artificial life support be discontinued. In other words, they should pull the plug.

While some are concerned that this document will be ignored by loved ones or the medical profession, some recent court decisions have upheld the individual's right to die. It is important to note that the Living Will is not necessarily a request to act, but rather a right to act. Only you or your family decides when it is time to use the living will. It can be stored at home with your will or living trust and other legal documents and you can make it available only to those you trust. Today, the right to die is a recognized right, and although some cases have recognized verbal statements, it is often required that you have expressed your wishes in writing. Some states require that living wills be re signed and dated and preferably witnessed every five years. Although the living will is still not recognized in New York, Massachusetts and Michigan, some people prepare them anyway, in anticipation of their acceptance. At the very least, it is important to tell those near to you what your life values are and how they should impact their decisions on your behalf if you become incapacitated.

Congress has recently passed legislation that requires all medical institutions, including nursing homes, to advise people entering the institutions of their right to advance directives. While it may be helpful to have this information at the time of admission, a better time to prepare such a document is when you are in good health—without the pressure of a serious illness distracting you.

With an Anatomical Gift Form, you can make a gift of your vital organs upon your death to help save other people's lives, or, you can donate your body to science for research and study. The anatomical gift form can be kept at home with your other legal documents and only revealed after your death. Although your organs may become less useful as you age, you should not worry whether you are too old to donate. Of course, those people who are not comfortable or willing to make a donation of this sort don't require such a document.

Tips for Creating a Comprehensive Advance Directive

1 Thoroughly think through your instructions and have discussions with family and friends in order to determine your values in regard to quality of life, comfort, and your ability to function.

2 Work with the Beliefs and Values sections that many standard forms offer to help you clarify your preferences.

3 Consider what things in life are important to you to make life worth living—what is worth sustaining, how you want to sustain it, and what is not worth sustaining.

4 Consider and write down what goals you have in life—is it to play golf, to see your grandchild graduate, to have just enough time to say goodbye to your loved ones should you become very ill suddenly?

5 Be as clear as possible about all of the options and decisions that you do have a right to be making. Consider the implications of different types of circumstances, treatments, and drugs.

- If communicating with loved ones is important to you, are you willing to take painkillers or other medications for comfort's sake that interfere with your ability to communicate adequately?
- If you enjoy a good meal, are you willing to live being fed through a tube in your stomach, or to take medications that make it difficult for you to swallow?
- If you like to be active, is it acceptable to you to be confined to a bed for the rest of your life?
- Is receiving shots several times a day something you can tolerate?
- In what circumstance would such things as tube feeding, artificial respiration and cardio-pulmonary resuscitation be acceptable?
- In what circumstances are you willing or not willing to accept hospitalization? Why would you or why would you not accept hospitalization?

▶ **Continued**

▶ Continued

6 Have thorough discussions with the person who you are appointing as your attorney in fact to ensure that they know what their responsibilities will be and to be sure they are comfortable with what you might be asking them to do.

7 Even if you have a written Advance Directive, it is impossible to cover every possibility. Therefore, talk to as many people as you can, including your health care practitioners, about your wishes and philosophies on these topics, so that if an emergency strikes, people can piece together easily and with agreement, what your true wishes might be.

8 Reevaluate your Living Will or Advance Directive on a regular basis and whenever any relevant change occurs in your family situation, physical condition, philosophy, values, tolerance, or finances.

9 Keep a copy of your Living Will or Advance Directive on file at your local hospital if you have a medical file there, and with your primary care physicians as well as with your family and Attorney in Fact.

10 When having any medical treatment, even minor outpatient treatment, always take a copy of your Advance Directive with you and make sure the staff is aware that you have it.

Source: Pat Kappas-Larson, V.P., Health Services and Dr. John Mach, Chief Medical Officer, EverCare, Minneapolis, Minnesota

I DON'T WANT TO ACHIEVE IMMORTALITY THROUGH WORK…I WANT TO ACHIEVE IT THROUGH NOT DYING.

—Woody allen

Since all aspects of your affairs overlap and affect each other, if you have different people assigned to take care of your health care decisions, your right-to-die and your financial affairs, be sure to state in each of the documents who has the last word on a decision, should there be disagreement between them.

Does having an Advance Directive guarantee that my true wishes will be carried out?

Situations in which your wishes may not or will not be fulfilled include:

- When you are in a state that does not recognize living wills or physicians directives.
- When you call 911 or are being treated by emergency medical staff. Emergency medical staff are not required to acknowledge a Living Will. Practically speaking, they often do not have time to stop to review and digest the finer details of your wishes, without risking your life. Your health care proxy or attorney in fact is also not likely to be present with the appropriate paperwork. Furthermore, often medical teams make decisions based on what they think will protect them from the legal system.
- When your Advance Directive is not readily available to your family, medical practitioners, or hospital.
- When the person(s) you assigned to make decisions on your behalf did not understand your wishes or has fundamental—even religious—differences that make it difficult or impossible for them to carry out your requests.
- When family members disagree and fight over what steps should be taken.
- Where, as required in some states, there are not two physicians who agree that you have a terminal condition or that you are sufficiently incapacitated to warrant your Attorney in Fact to take over decision making powers.
- When your wishes have changed, perhaps due to some change in circumstances, and you have not updated your Advance Directive to reflect those changes.
- When you have not thoroughly thought out the details and specifics of your wishes, such that the spirit of your intentions is not represented in the Living Will.

WHAT COUNTS IS NOT THE YEARS IN YOUR LIFE BUT THE LIFE IN YOUR YEARS.

—Adlai Stevenson

How can I communicate my wishes for burial and memorial?

Use a memorial letter to communicate burial and memorial wishes to your family and friends.

A **Memorial Letter** could contain your specific or general wishes concerning burial or cremation, suggestions for the type of memorial service you would want or what charitable contributions in your honor you would like survivors to make. You can leave as much detail as you like—what music you want played or what poem read, for instance. These preferences are usually expressed as wishes rather than commands as you don't want to dictate anything that might come into conflict with your will or trust.

Your memorial letter should be kept in a place where it can be easily and immediately locted, not locked in a safe deposit box that may not be opened until long after your funeral. Your church may even keep it on file for you.

Memorial Service Checklist

- Location
- Who to invite
- Who will speak
- Readings
- Music
- Flowers or decorations
- Favorite photograph
- Food
- Published obituary text

Should I seek assistance in creating an estate plan?

There are very few benefits of doing your own estate planning, except perhaps savings in up-front costs. These savings, however, will most likely be lost by having an estate plan that is less than adequate.

Settling an estate can be a very complicated matter, and preparing properly for that can also be a complicated matter. It requires expertise and experience that the average citizen does not have. There are many negative aspects of preparing your own estate plan, including the possibility that your wishes will not be carried out and that your estate will have to pay unnecessary estate taxes or probate fees.

Who can help me with estate planning?

Start by selecting a lawyer who is an estate planning specialist, then identify the other advisors for your team.

No matter who else you work with, a lawyer is an essential player on the estate planning team. This is the best place to start—with an estate planning lawyer. He or she will review your personal situation and help you to decide what other advisors you should have join the team. Other professionals who may have a role to play on your estate planning team include:

Most people do not need to work with all of these advisors, but some estate planning may require cooperative efforts between those advisors who are necessary and who you do choose to work with. One of the most important points to remember is that the team you put together should be able to work together in harmony toward the realization of your goals.

Seek recommendations from people and sources you trust to make sure you are working with the right advisors. Then place fact-finding phone calls and have initial consultations. (See page 103 for tips for choosing your advisors.)

How do I choose a lawyer?

The First Thing to Ask

Some lawyers limit their practice to big estates only. You can ask about limits early in your conversation to make sure you are not wasting your time.

Schedule a phone or face-to-face interview to choose a lawyer.

Ask the following questions:

How long have you been in practice? While it is not the only criterion, many years of experience can be valuable in any profession.

Do you do estate planning? Is it your specialty, or part of a broader law practice? What percentage of the practice is devoted to estate planning? The other areas of law that are closely related to estate planning include tax law, planned charitable giving, business succession planning, and probate work. If the attorney practices in other, unrelated areas, such as criminal defense or medical malpractice, he or she may not have the estate planning experience that you need.

If you have an interest in a particular type of estate planning, such as a living trust, for instance, ask the attorney if he or she uses it as an estate planning tool. Some areas such as these require special knowledge and experience, and you are better off working with someone who is very familiar with them.

Do you also write wills? What proportion of wills to living trusts do you do in your practice? These questions will help you to determine how oriented the attorney is toward avoiding probate court

Do you carry malpractice insurance? This insurance is designed to cover losses to you and your heirs or beneficiaries which occur through attorney mistakes or negligence.

Do you limit your clientele by size of estate or amount of wealth? Some lawyers do this and it will save you time to know this up front. If your estate does not fall within his or her range and you like the attorney, ask for a referral to another attorney.

On average, how long does it take to prepare an estate plan? The average plan should not take more than 2 to 4 weeks to complete, assuming you have all the information available.

Is there a charge for an initial consultation? If so, how much is it? Is there a charge if I bring along my old estate planning documents for your review? There are attorneys who do not charge for the initial consultation, even with old estate plan documents to review. However, it is not unfair or unusual if there is a charge. Just be sure you know how much it will be and what your consultation will cover.

How do you determine the fee you will charge for an estate plan? What you need to find out is whether it is a flat fee or an hourly fee. It would be too soon, in the first phone call, to ask for an actual fee quote from the attorney. However, it would be fair to expect a quote during the initial consultation after the attorney has reviewed all of your documents, including any questionnaires she or he might have given you to fill out, and determined what you want to accomplish with your estate plan.

Do you have expertise in federal estate tax planning? If your estate might exceed the estate tax exemption ($675,000 in the year 2000—see chart on page 29), this would be an important question to ask.

Is your fee/service agreement in writing and when would my payments be due? Are there any additional expenses I could expect? Legal fee agreements should always be in writing with clear terms for any payment schedule. Legitimate add-ons, such as the cost of transferring deeds, should be disclosed to you, and you should be informed whenever there are charges for optional, extra services not included in the flat or hourly fee quoted by the lawyer.

Do you maintain ongoing contact with your clients? Will you advise me of updates in estate or trust law, or remind me when it is time to review my planning documents? You might also want to know in what form this contact occurs.

Experience Counts

Choosing a lawyer with expertise in estate planning will make the process easier.

Get it in Writing

Make sure you get details about costs and payment terms in writing. This will eliminate surprises later.

What do I need to do for my initial meeting with a lawyer?

Be prepared.

Once you have made your investigative phone calls or interviews and have found an attorney whom you think might be satisfactory, you should meet for an initial consultation. To get the most from that consultation:

- Set aside at least 2 hours for your first meeting.
- If you are married, be sure to take your spouse with you. If you arrive without your spouse, most lawyers will realize they will have to explain everything a second time and that changes may have to be made once the second spouse becomes part of the process.
- It might be advisable to have one or more of your other advisors present for the meeting.
- Take whatever documents the lawyer has requested.
- Expect to answer questions about your assets, yourself, your family, your objectives, and your current estate plan, if you have one. To do the very best job for you, the attorney should ask you many questions. (If you had give permission to the attorney to talk to any of your advisors ahead of time, it will cut down on the number of questions you must answer.)
- Don't hide assets from the attorney because you think it will keep your legal fees down. A non-disclosed asset will become a problem at some point during your lifetime or afterward.
- Ask questions. You are not expected to know everything already. If you did, you would not need to hire an attorney!
- Be prepared to make decisions about the guardianship of any dependents, how you want your estate distributed, making charitable gifts, disinheriting any heirs and naming any trustees.
- Be prepared, at the conclusion of the initial consultation to pay all or part of the lawyer's fee, unless he or she indicates otherwise.
- Set a definite date for your follow-up appointment for the execution (signing) of your documents. Set aside 2 to 3 hours for this appointment.
- You will have to fund any trusts you create—that is—transfer your property's titles into their name. If you do not wish to do that yourself, you will have to provide your attorney with the deeds and titles.

To create a customized estate plan, you may need to consult other professionals.

Over the course of your work with your lawyer to create your customized estate plan, he or she may make suggestions concerning the purchase of insurance, the use or distribution of property, or other steps that can further your estate planning objectives. If you have not already done so, this would be an appropriate time to consult your other advisors or ask your lawyer or trusted friends or colleagues for referrals.

What role can an insurance agent play? In estate planning, insurance is often referred to as the fuel (the cash) that runs the vehicle (your plan). Even if you have a large estate, it may have poor liquidity—that is, it may be difficult to transfer your property into cash. Leaving an estate cash poor can cause no end of difficulties. Insurance, depending on the type, can both protect your estate while you are still living and provide the cash needed to cover a variety of costs and expenses after you die. There are three primary areas of insurance that are relevant to estate planning:

- **Health insurance**—Without health insurance, any serious illness could not only bring about bankruptcy, but your estate could be seriously diminished, if not destroyed.
- **Long-term care insurance**—An extended disability requiring long-term care can also wipe out an estate very quickly. This insurance helps pay for nurses and other expenses involved in your care during a long-term illness or disability.
- **Life insurance**—Life insurance helps provide liquidity to your estate, after you have died. It can provide money to pay estate taxes, if necessary, and other death related expenses such as probate fees and funeral expenses. It can also help replace your income so that your family is not left stranded. There are decisions that have to be made, such as who the beneficiaries should be, what kind of policy you need, and what amount of coverage you need.

Where do other professionals fit in?

Choosing an Insurance Agent

To determine if an insurance agent is someone you want to join your team, find out:

- If the agent represents a single insurance company or several. Ask for company annual report and check their financial rating with Moody's or Standard and Poor's.
- If the agent is a generalist or a specialist. It could be useful if he or she is a generalist but knows all insurance products well. However, if he or she is a specialist in the insurance that you need, this might be the route to take.
- What knowledge or training the agent has on the estate planning process and the cooperative role other professionals play in that process. A good agent will talk honestly with you about his or her philosophy of teamwork. Not all agents will have extensive experience but all should be enthusiastic and knowledgeable on the subject.
- Is the agent willing to do extra work for you? Agents are paid on commission, not hourly. Less conscientious agents might not go the extra mile for you and your estate plan once they've made the sale.

Getting Other Help

Choosing a CPA

- Does he or she specialize in estate planning, estate taxes, trust taxation or fiduciary compliance? Yes to any of these questions is good.
- Is he or she willing to work with your attorney over the phone or in a meeting? Ask what the fee would be for this.

Choosing a CFP

- The planner's background, education and experience.
- What she or he will do to accommodate your estate planning objectives.
- If the CFP is a specialist in any area. Ask how she or he would balance your plan.
- How the CFP is compensated. There are three methods for payment–fee only, commission only, or fee and commission. The fee only is probably the best as the CFP will not stand to gain or lose commission based on your choices.
- How the CFP will work with you. Will there be regular meetings and if so, how often?

Choosing a Stock Broker

- How many years of experience he or she has. Look for someone who has not moved around to many different firms. Look at the broker's formal education and professional licenses.
- If she or he has references from people with similar investment needs as yours as well as people with greater and lesser risk tolerance than yours.
- How she or he will manage your investment accounts. Ask the stockbroker to explain which investments produce the most income for her/him.

What role can a Certified Public Accountant (CPA) play? Your CPA is someone who should have or gain immediate familiarity with your current income and tax situation, and can advise you of potential tax problems and their solutions before they arise. CPAs are well trained and have passed rigorous qualifying examinations. Ideally your CPA should be attuned to the importance of tax strategies as they relate to estate planning.

What role can a Certified Financial Planner (CFP) play? A CFP can help you to clarify your goals, set priorities, and manage your assets now to increase their value. You will want someone who is able to include your estate planning objectives along with your life and lifestyle objectives when guiding you through the many financial decisions that you will have to make over the coming years.

What role can a Stockbroker play? You can work with a stockbroker to invest in your retirement, your children's college education, government securities, precious metals, and sometimes commodities. Everyone has different risk tolerance levels, and the best stockbroker will work with you at your level. A good stockbroker can recommend modified investment strategies that are compatible with your overall estate planning objectives, while still allowing you to take the appropriate risks.

Where do I fit into the picture? Every team needs a coach and that is where you fit in. That means you make the decisions by setting out your estate planning objectives—which in turn define the plan which should be put into effect by your team.

General Tips for Choosing Your Advisors

When you place the call and first meet the professional, you should note:

1. How are you treated and greeted? The staff reflects their professionalism.

2. Is your telephone call immediately transferred to them or do you feel as if you are being screened? While there can be legitimate reasons for screening calls, you should never be made to feel as if the purpose of the screening is to determine whether you are "important" or not.

3. If they are not available, do you receive a return phone call within a timely fashion? The staff should be able to tell you approximately when they will return your call, and if they can't call on time, the staff should call to tell you so.

4. Do they listen and not just talk? Are they courteous or are your conversations interrupted by calls or office business? The advisor's attitude toward your conversation may reveal what his or her attitude toward your estate plan might be.

5. When you visit, how does their work environment look? Their environment can tell you a lot about their professionalism and whether you will be able to relate well with them.

6. Do they take time to answer all of your questions? They won't always have the time to answer all of your questions in the first phone call. If not, they should tactfully let you know that their phone time is limited. You can then ask for a first consultation which is often free of charge. If you can't get all of your questions answered within a reasonable time, you might seek someone else who has more time for you.

7. Do they ask you questions in order to give you the best information? While there are some generalities in estate planning, it is difficult to discuss your particular situation without knowing some personal facts.

8. Do they use a lot of jargon that you can't understand or talk down to you? If so, they might not be the best for you.

9. Do they see the big picture of your estate plan or just the immediate payoff? You want a professional who can view your overall needs, both now and in the future.

10. Are they more interested in selling something than in meeting your needs? Advisors should earn their income by providing you with good service, and not by selling you anything you will buy.

11. Does it seem to you that they would like to have you as a client? If not, they may also not be motivated to give your estate plan the attention it needs.

12. Do you like them and feel you will be comfortable in a long term relationship? Since you will need to be regularly updating and adjusting your estate plan and all other matters related to it, you could be working with them for many years.

13. Are they willing and eager to work with your other advisors to both improve your lifestyle and meet your estate planning goals? You need a team to work with, and therefore you need team players.

How much will I have to pay?

Costs vary greatly for the preparation and maintenance of your estate plan.

How much you will pay depends on how many elements your plan involves, the rates your lawyer charges, and the area of the country you live in. The cost can also be affected by the breadth and the depth of the services you need. There are many different levels of service, and those attorneys offering the most comprehensive service will likely be the most expensive.

The cost can range from as low as $250 for a will with a small-town general practice lawyer, to many thousands of dollars for a complicated plan for a large estate prepared by a high-powered big-city law firm.

Living trusts, given the many variables, might range in cost from $1,700 to $3,200 (the approximate equivalent of probate fees your estate would otherwise have to pay if it ranged in size from $20,000 to $50,000).

The costs vary for estate planning tools such as Irrevocable Life Insurance Trusts or Charitable Remainder Trusts. You are best advised to obtain quotations specifically from the lawyers you interview.

It is important to note that while the initial costs of creating an estate plan may seem high, they are very small compared to the cost of probate and, in the case of larger estates, any unnecessary taxes paid. A good estate plan saves your estate money.

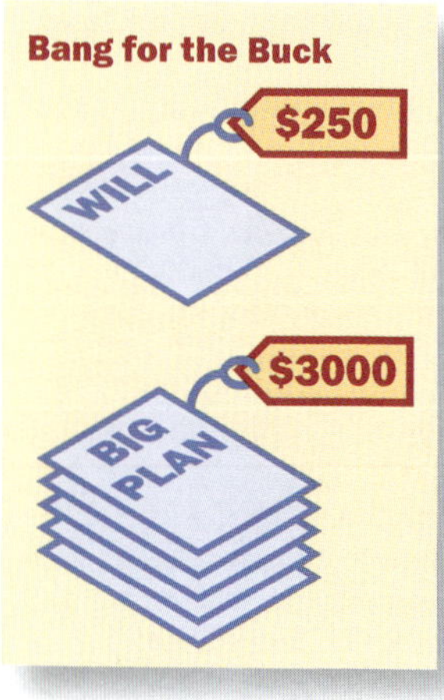

Economy does not lie in sparing money but in spending it wisely.

—T.H. Huxley

Begin preparing your estate plan by gathering information and making decisions.

Identify and make a list of assets and liabilities. Potential assets could include not only the obvious such as real estate and your car, but also insurance policies, debts owed to you, and retirement plans, for instance. Liabilities include all moneys you owe including such debts as personal loans from family members (see page 34).

Note the form of ownership or form of title for each asset and the percentage you own (See page 36).

Evaluate potential tax and probate liabilities (see page 28).

Decide who should benefit from the estate. Do you have children or grandchildren you want to provide for, or a favorite friend or charity you want to remember?

Decide on alternate plans, should you both you and your spouse die at the same time. You can avoid many complications later if you plan for this possibility now.

Decide who should be the alternate beneficiaries, should you outlive your beneficiaries. It is not unusual for a person who has been chosen as a beneficiary to die before the will maker or trust maker. If you do not decide this now, should the beneficiary die before you, you will have to change your will or trust to make it most effective.

How do I get started in creating an estate plan?

You should begin planning your estate as soon as you have any assets or responsibilities such as a business or a family.

Alternative Beneficiaries

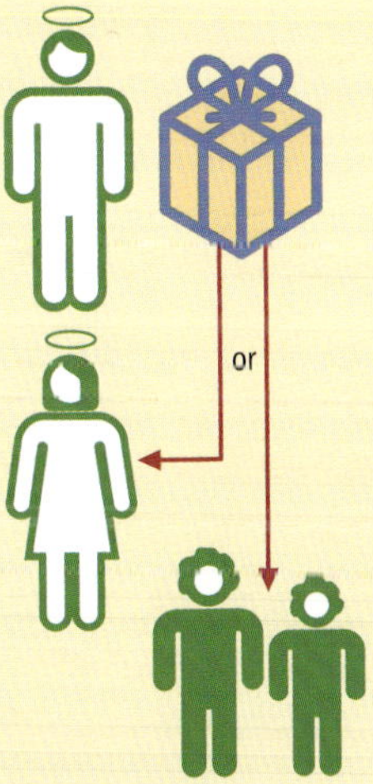

Designate alternative beneficiaries in case your primary beneficiary dies before you.

When They're Ready

You may want your beneficiaries to receive their inheritance only when they have reached a specific age or other conditions have been met. Your executor or trustee can manage the assets in the meantime.

Decide when your beneficiaries should benefit from your estate and any restrictions that should be on the gifts. Do you want your beneficiary to receive their inheritance immediately upon your death? Do you want them to wait until they are a certain age, or married or in college? Do you want to maintain any kind of control over the gift after your death? Your decisions here will determine the best estate planning tools to use to accomplish your goals.

Determine which assets should go toward payment of debts or any estate taxes you expect. This is an important decision to make in advance. If you have not already arranged it, life insurance or a life insurance trust can provide ready cash to pay debts as well as support your survivors. If you don't specify which assets should be liquidated, if necessary, to pay debts, then your estate plan is incomplete and may not be carried out the way you intended.

Determine which companion documents are needed or if changes to existing documents are needed (see pages 56 and 68).

Select the guardians of any minor or dependent children and provide detailed instructions for them.

Provide for your pets and their care.

In the case of living trusts, arrange for the transfer of your assets into the name of the trust. This is called funding the trust (see page 64).

Select trustees and/or executors and determine their responsibilities and powers (see page 7).

How do I maintain my estate plan?

Consult your attorney and other estate planning team members periodically.

Once your estate plan is complete, consult with your attorney periodically to update and make changes to your trusts or will as circumstances dictate. Difficult situations can arise if you die with an estate plan that has not been updated. For instance, you may have left cash or property that you no longer own at the time of death to a beneficiary. How this situation is resolved will depend on how a court interprets the intent of your estate plan. Under the doctrines of ademption, the person will not receive it and may not receive anything else in its stead. It is possible, however, that other assets in your estate that you left to other beneficiaries might have to be liquidated to ensure that an equivalent cash gift is given. If your estate plan makes more cash gifts than there is cash, an **abatement** would be required.

While the thought of undertaking the tasks on this list may seem overwhelming, imagine how much easier it is for you to do it than it would be for your survivors after you die.

Abatement means reducing all the gifts when there isn't enough to go around.

IT IS GOOD TO HAVE MONEY AND THE THINGS THAT MONEY CAN BUY, BUT IT'S GOOD, TOO, TO CHECK UP ONCE IN A WHILE AND MAKE SURE YOU HAVEN'T LOST THE THINGS THAT MONEY CAN'T BUY.

—George Horace Lorimer

How do I deal with the emotional aspect of estate planning?

Estate planning involves money, whether it is cash or property. As many of us learn, wherever money is involved, emotions can run high and disagreements are common.

One of the purposes of an estate plan is to reduce the addition of negative emotions to already difficult circumstances for your survivors when you die. It is not unusual for people to view estate planning as a morbid or uncomfortable topic. It involves letting go of one's possessions and perhaps working through deep emotions. Unresolved family issues may arise, with old memories and regrets pushing to the forefront. Like other aspects of the death process, it's very common to avoid planning until it is too late to do it well. Consulting a minister, rabbi or other counselor, or even your doctor might help you understand what is making you feel so uneasy about the estate planning process.

Ask your friends to assist you or perhaps to be actively involved in the process to ease your anxiety. It helps if you can focus on all the good things you will be doing for your beneficiaries and see it as an extension of your financial plan.

Chapter **10**

How do I share my wishes with others?

Be prepared by having a good grasp on the details of your plan.

If your plan is already in place and you are happy with it, you will want to have a good grasp on the details of the plan and the reasoning behind it, so that you can offer valid explanations for your decisions. It is also helpful if you can first learn any sensitivities a particular family member might have so that you can address those in the best possible way. If you have not yet established a plan, you will want to determine what questions you need answered to best help you to develop the kind of plan you want.

When should I discuss my plans and wishes? If you have not discussed your plans, you should do so as soon as possible, especially if you want to have discussions before you establish your estate plan. Your timing is important, particularly if you think that the loved one will not be in agreement with your wishes. Set aside a relaxed time, when other activities or people are not going to interfere and make an effort to explain your plans and wishes, if necessary. If possible, meet in person because you may be covering some sensitive ground.

How do I begin the conversation? One easy way would be to mention that you had read this book recently and that it suggested that you speak with relevant parties about your estate plans. Or you can use a major life change, such as retirement, a milestone birthday, or the death of a relative to naturally bring up the subject. No matter what your estate plans are, it can be a compliment to others that you wish to share your plans with them. Begin by telling them why you want to discuss your plans with them.

When it comes to money, family loyalty goes out the window. They are just people dividing money.

—Jeffrey L. Dondon

Questions to Ask Yourself

- To whom do I want to talk? It can be advisable, for instance, to talk with those you wish to have as guardians for your dependents, or as executors or trustees. Although, not everyone may be comfortable doing this, especially if one family member has been chosen over another for these roles. It is possible that tension could be generated among family members. As years go by, it is also possible that you might want to be able to change who fills these positions without hurting anybody's feelings.

- What should I talk about? Do you want to tell them about your decisions or ask them for suggestions or advice? Do you want to discuss the mechanics of how your estate plan will work?

- Do I want to give my trustees and beneficiaries copies of my estate plan? Again, this is strictly a personal decision. It is not necessary to do so if for any reason you are uncomfortable with it. But, after your death, prior conversations will have helped ensure less confusion about what your wishes were.

Who should I talk to and in what order?

Communication among family members about your estate plan is a healthy process which can help to relieve tension later. However, in some cases, raising the subject will raise old conflicts and create tension. Some people may also be afraid that such discussions will reveal qualities they don't want to see in their loved ones, like greed or a lack of compassion. Ultimately, only you can decide whether, when, and how to talk about your plans.

Some families hold family retreats, even if it is just to work out who gets which personal item. Sometimes if you don't discuss it, you really don't know which of your belongings your heirs and beneficiaries would prefer. There are a few estate planning attorneys who are pioneering **multi-generation cooperative planning** where parents, adult children and even adult grandchildren all come together with the attorney in retreats and work out everyone's plans so that a mutually-desired goal can be reached. When there are unresolved family issues, these sessions can even be facilitated by a counselor. If the estate is very large (over $5 million, for instance) these retreats can last an entire weekend.

There are some people who may not feel that talking is the answer, as it sometimes only further highlights irreconcilable differences. If for some reason you do not wish to explain your decisions in person, or if you have tried with no success, you could write a thorough explanation of why you made the choices you did and include it with your estate plan to be read and contemplated later, after your death.

Is it necessary for me to reveal my estate plan to my children and other beneficiaries?

If you are leaving your estate to your heirs in a fairly equitable way and they all are compatible, then discussing your estate plans, even in detail, will probably be a pleasant experience. If you don't feel comfortable going into great detail, or getting them involved, at least forewarning them that an estate plan exists is a good idea so that if you were to die suddenly, they would know to look for it.

Look at needs realistically.

Many estate planning advisors recommend that you take an honest look at the realistic needs of your loved ones and plan from there. How old are your children? What kind of education are they accustomed to? What kind of help would you want to give them in their adulthood were you to continue living? What about your spouse? How much has she or he depended upon you? The issue of non-working women often comes up. Of course, non-working does not mean that a woman has not worked—it just means that she has worked and not received a paycheck. Preparing in your estate plan to provide for a woman who has dedicated herself to work without pay might be viewed as preparing to provide her with a well-deserved pension and retirement fund. In many families, women have sacrificed their own careers for the family and subsequently have not been able to build their skills, experience, and resumés sufficiently to get a position that would pay adequately upon the death of their husbands. If that woman still has children at home, it can be even more of a hardship as she would then have to keep two jobs—mother/homemaker and wage-earner. For many estate planning professionals, providing for a widow who has worked in the home is a top priority, together with insuring stability for any dependents.

How do I determine the needs of my beneficiaires?

YOU CAN NEVER PLAN THE FUTURE BY THE PAST.

—EDMUND BURKE

Career moms often have more marketable skills than stay-at-home moms. A well-developed estate plan will find ways to provide for one who has sacrificed a career for the unpaid work of running a household.

You cannot accurately predict the future. Make the best assessment of the unique characteristics of your beneficiaries and plan as well as you can. You can't anticipate every possibility.

How do I make a plan that works for my heirs? Most people want to leave a legacy that really works for their heirs and beneficiaries. While focusing on the technicalities of estate planning and the satisfactions your gifts will bring your beneficiaries, it is important not to overlook any conditions or circumstances and known human dynamics that might interfere with how your estate plan works after you have died. Many estate planning professionals would say that your plan won't succeed unless you take human concerns into consideration. Of course, sometimes what you think works for your beneficiaries is not always what they think is going to work for them—particularly in cases where you feel that you need to exert some kind of control over your gifts after you die, and the beneficiary is a fully grown adult. Before starting your planning, it is important to assess your personal circumstances and consider how you want to handle conflicting needs. And when making an estate plan, it is very important to take into consideration the personalities, traits, strengths, weaknesses and relationships of your beneficiaries and then plan accordingly. Otherwise, your plans may not really work for everyone as you intended.

How do I handle it when there are changes in my beneficiary's situation after I have made my estate plan? If the changes are drastic enough, then you may want to make changes in your estate plan. If you have already told the beneficiary about a gift and you change it later, it would only be fair to let them know of the change and the reason for it, since they might be including it in their long term planning. If you haven't revealed anything to them, then you do not necessarily have to reveal the change either.

Surprise Them

Think carefully about revealing the larger gifts you intend to make to a beneficiary. There is the danger that those gifts will not be available later due to some unforeseen circumstance or a change of heart. You will then be in the uncomfortable position of rescinding the promise, which they may already have banked on.

Listen and offer explanations...seek counsel if necessary.

How do I plan what I want to do versus what others think I should do? It is never a bad idea to listen to what those near and dear, as well as what professional advisors have to say about plans you are making. The more knowledgeable you are, the better able you are to make good decisions. Ultimately, however, it is your estate and it is up to you to decide who you want to leave what to and how. If you do care about the feelings of those who disagree, it would help if you offered them an explanation for your final decision, verbally, or in writing.

How do I address any guilt I may feel? Often people feel guilty about some decision they are making in their estate planning process. Perhaps they have a favorite brother who happens to be irresponsible with money, so making him executor of your estate is a bad idea. Or perhaps a sister adores your daughter but you know she would make a very poor guardian. In some ways, guilt can serve to give us a message that we need to change an attitude or something we are feeling or doing. However, what it is exactly that we need to change is often not what we are feeling guilty about. Unfortunately other people can often see our guilt before we do, and some even know how to use it to their advantage. If you know that the choices you are making in your estate plan are good and right but you still feel guilty, you might want to seek counsel with a trusted friend or counselor to get to the root of it.

How can I deal with pressures put on me by my loved ones? In situations like this, it helps to be very clear about what your plans are and why you have chosen those plans. Depending on how big an issue it becomes between you and those close to you, involving a mediator can also be useful.

How do I deal with pressures and guilt?

It can be a good idea to speak with your attorney, financial planners or other counselors to help you develop a method for educating others as to the good reasons for your decisions. You can even do this in advance, if you foresee that someone will be applying pressure. If the person putting the pressure on you is near and dear, it may be worthwhile to have them meet with your attorney or other estate planning professionals who can provide further education.

What about specific bequests?

Gifts may be equal, unequal, or shared.

How do I make my gifts equal? If you truly intend to make your gifts equal, it means simply evaluating the cash value of your various properties and then dividing up the property equally between your beneficiaries such that the total value of what they each receive is equal. Where some properties are not readily marketable, the beneficiaries may also prefer that the estate sell the properties and then distribute the proceeds. It does make sense to know if your beneficiaries have preferences as to whether they would prefer that cash value, or what property they would like to have. If they all want the same things, then you might have to find some way to allow them to share the ownership. Of course, if you have spent more on one child during your life, you may want to equalize your gifts by taking into account any large differences in the money you spent on the children before your death. Remember that asset values do change. In order to maintain equality of your gifts, you should review your estate plan with your attorney every one or two years.

How do I handle unequal gifts? Some attorneys do not encourage parents to leave unequal gifts to children. Sometimes when parents do, they leave more to their unsuccessful children and less to the successful, which seems to be rewarding lack of success and punishing success. But often unequal gifts make more sense to parents than equal gifts. Beneficiaries all have different needs and different circumstances. One daughter, for instance, could be happily married to a wealthy husband with no children, while another daughter could be the single mother of two. Or, you may have spent much more on one child than another during your life. For instance, you may have spent $200,000 putting one child through medical school while the other children earned scholarships or went to inexpensive local community colleges. If you were not to take this into account, the children may feel it is unfair.

If you are comfortable with it, discussing unequal gifts up front with your beneficiaries can be a good idea. The one receiving the lesser gift might be counting on receiving an equal share and may be making decisions based on that—his or her disappointment could be lessened if he or she had not been counting on it for years. It also gives you an opportunity to reassure them that you love them all equally. If, however, you feel you cannot discuss it with them, a detailed letter offering the reasons for your choices with reassurances of your love can be included with your estate plan.

How do I handle shared gifts? Sometimes beneficiaries are all determined to receive the same particular item. It might be property—a summer cottage for instance—or a beloved set of family portraits that have a sentimental value. In these cases, allowing beneficiaries to share the property might be the best solution. They could time-share the cottage and perhaps rotate the portraits annually. You might offer some neutral method that they can use to determine in what order the rotation occurs—drawing straws, for instance. While leaving gifts to share has its complications, the beneficiaries might prefer those complications to giving up the gift entirely.

How do I address the complications of divorce and second marriages? People who marry more than once may face problems reconciling their wishes for their present spouse and family with their wishes for children from a previous marriage. Discussing your plans with your spouse and children (if they are adult) is a good idea if you feel that they will respond reasonably. If the children carry any resentment over your later marriage or other related issues, it might be better not to discuss your plans and just leave a detailed explanation with your estate plan. There are many ways you can work with trusts to allow your spouse to retain the use and income of your property after you have died, but such that the property passes to your children upon his or her death.

If the terms and conditions of loans to beneficiaries are not written anywhere, the confusion that could ensue after your death could create strife and unpleasantness with other beneficiaries. To solve this problem, keep a record with your estate plan of the terms of any loans.

Dealing with Beneficiaries Who Owe You Money

When your heirs or beneficiaries owe you money, that debt will become an asset of your estate. You can choose, if you so wish, to include the forgiveness of that debt in your plan as part of your gift to that beneficiary. But you should seek legal advise on this, because such a gift requires special handling. If you are forgiving a debt that is substantially greater than what you are leaving to your other beneficiaries, you might run into some resistance and anger, since the other beneficiaries will perceive that a portion of their rightful inheritance has gone to another beneficiary.

Forgive Us Our Debts...

If you were married when you made a loan, you may only own half of the debt, and therefore have the right to forgive only half the debt.

If you omit a child from your estate plan, consider writing a letter telling the child what you are doing and why. On the other hand, if you think it might make things worse, you might want to leave the letter for them to read after your death.

If you omit a child from your estate plan, there is a chance that that child will sue or become a burden to his or her siblings. Consider instead leaving a trust with specifications as to when and how the child will receive money or income from the trust.

Rather than disinherit heirs, some people just leave a small amount in their wills and then include a "no-contest" clause. This is a clause that states that if any beneficiary challenges a will, they get nothing if their challenge is not successful.

If your children die, their children become your legal heirs in their stead. If you wish to disinherit these grandchildren, you must also do so in your will just as you would your own children.

How do I disinherit heirs? Some parents want to disinherit a child or a grandchild (the children of any deceased children are also heirs) while others just want to protect their property from the child's relations or friends. It is legal to disinherit a child, if you do it properly in a will. Just leaving their name out of a will or trust is not sufficient, as the state will just view them as forgotten (or pretermitted) heirs and provide them with a share of your estate equal to any other children or according to state law. You have to specifically state that you are disinheriting the child, or simply leave them a small bequest. If you don't include children in your will because you are providing for them from outside the will—in a living trust, life insurance or a joint tenancy, for instance—you still must expressly exclude them in the will if there is any chance they might take advantage of the pretermitted child laws. To discourage the child from contesting your will, it helps if you offer an explanation so that it does not appear to be a mistake or oversight. If the reason you wish to disinherit an heir is because of concerns about their friends or relations, you might consider establishing a trust that imposes certain restrictions on how the bequest is provided to the heir. Disinheriting a spouse can be more difficult. If you live in one of the 41 common-law states (see page 40) you cannot disinherit your spouse. In the nine community property states, however, where both spouses equally share the marital property, it is possible to leave your half of the estate to whomever you choose and to exclude your spouse, if you so wish.

How do I leave gifts to non-family? Since non-family members are definitely not heirs, they will not receive anything unless you specifically leave it to them in a will or a trust. Since your family members might be expecting the property themselves, it helps if you can forewarn them and let them get used to the idea. The more explanation you can offer, the easier it might be for them to accept it without ill feelings. Failing that, offering a reason in writing with the bequest will help avoid hurt feelings.

How do I encourage loved ones to plan for their estates?

Seize an opportunity to talk about the subject.

According to the American Association of Retired Persons, most adult children do not know much about their parents' estate or financial planning. And many children are sensitive about asking their parents for fear of the negative reaction that might result from the inquiry. However, a lack of knowledge will certainly create not only anxiety but the probability of inefficiency and greater cost when an emergency arises. Don't wait until concerns about poor health arise. You should also remember that a discussion of your parent's estate planning needs may affect your own estate planning, and you may need to consider revising your own strategies.

It can be uncomfortable to sit down with a parent, or spouse, and talk about death. There may be lots of love and trust, but in terms of disclosing financial information, there is an element of privacy people feel. So, how do you begin? You can use a major life change, such as retirement, a milestone birthday or the death of a relative to naturally bring up the subject. Another approach is to ask questions such as, have you done any estate planning or are there any estate decisions that I need to be aware of? Or asking your parents for estate planning advise can lead to a discussion of their own plans. One couple's daughter brought up the subject by suggesting that they consider giving more to her siblings, since she was doing so well. Once the topic was opened, the couple realized that they had to get going on their estate plan. Another approach would be to recruit a family member or close family friend who is closer in age to the loved ones to raise the subject first.

Once the topic is opened, the questions do not have to initially focus on financial issues or on what individual beneficiaries will receive. Instead, the questions should focus on understanding the overall wishes of a parent and how you can help. A very legitimate question to ask is who do you want to handle your affairs if you cannot? After they answer, they

Talk About It

Find a way to start the conversation. If no plan is in place, it's time to get going.

can be asked if their will and power of attorney reflect these wishes.

Adult children can ease the discussion about money by divulging information about their own finances first. This openness may make it easier for your parents to share financial information. Stay away from questions about the size of their assets, and focus instead on the location of the related paperwork.

Be sure that one or more of the children has access to their safe deposit box and/or knows the combination to their home safe. You should also know the names of their accountant and attorney. And if they keep their records on their computer, find out what the password is in case you need to gain access to the programs for record-keeping.

Just knowing where these things are is critical. If such disclosures continue to make your parents uncomfortable, have them fill out a financial inventory worksheet. You could take a simple spiral notebook and have them list key information, such as the location and account numbers of life insurance policies, savings accounts, mutual funds or other items. Make sure you know the location of wills and insurance policies, safe deposit boxes and the names and addresses of attorneys and other professional people with whom your parents work. They don't even have to show the worksheet to you. But be sure to ask them where it can be found in case of an emergency. If your parents do give the form to you, make four copies. Give one to your parents and one to their lawyer or executor, place one in a safe deposit box, and keep a copy for yourself.

Once people understand that unless their affairs are properly planned the government will get more, they often become very interested in finding out what they should do to keep the government from getting whatever they have. While in your discussions you may discover that most things are in order, usually there are loose ends that need attention and, oftentimes, a lot of work is necessary to implement what parents want to have happen with the minimum of time and expense. Whatever tactic you take, you will be doing them and their families and loved ones a great service.

My interest is in the future because I am going to spend the rest of my life there.

—Charles F. Kettering

Index

T

U

V

W

Our Thanks

Sidney D. Kirkpatrick III and **Nancy Webster-Thurlbeck** for their research and writing contributions.

Don Moyer and the team at **Agnew Moyer Smith** for their talent in information architecture.

Sharon McRee and **Galen Griepp**, Attorneys and Counselors at law, for the ongoing editorial and advisory role that they played in the preparation of this book.

JoAnn Daudt, Attorney at Law, **Dunkley, Bennett & Christensen, P.A.**, for her editorial help.

Barry Webster, Barrister and Solicitor, for his contributions to this book.

Lette, Lette & partners, International Estate Planners.

John Mach, M.D., Medical Director, **Ovations Division, UnitedHealth Group**, Minneapolis.

Pat Kappas-Larson, Vice President Health Services, **Evercare Division, UnitedHealth Group**, Minneapolis.